What We Leave Behind

Samantha Rhodes

Published by Samantha Rhodes, 2024.

WHAT WE LEAVE BEHIND

First edition. July 22, 2024.

Copyright © 2024 Samantha Rhodes.

ISBN: 979-8224768936

Written by Samantha Rhodes.

Table of Contents

To those who have come before us and those who will follow, this book is dedicated to the eternal journey of leaving a lasting impact. May we honor the wisdom and values passed down through generations and strive to create a legacy that uplifts, inspires, and enlightens future generations. May our actions today shape a better tomorrow for all.

Preface

IN THE QUIET MOMENTS before dawn, standing at the edge of a calm lake, one can feel the weight of the world balanced on the horizon. The soft glow of the sunrise reflects not just on the water, but in the depths of our souls, casting light on the shadows of our lives. It is in these moments of introspection that we begin to contemplate the essence of our existence and the legacy we leave behind.

"What We Leave Behind" explores the intricate tapestry of our lives, woven with the threads of our actions, decisions, and the emotional imprints we bestow upon others. This book delves into the duality of our legacy: the tangible and the intangible, the visible and the unseen.

Personal Legacy and Life Reflections

THROUGHOUT OUR LIVES, we are constantly crafting a narrative—one that is unique to each of us yet universally relatable. This narrative is not merely a collection of events but a complex interplay of our choices, values, and the relationships we forge. As we navigate the journey of life, we often ponder how we will be remembered and the mark we will leave on the world.

In these pages, you will encounter stories of individuals who have grappled with their mortality and the desire to leave a meaningful legacy. These reflections offer insights into how everyday actions, seemingly small and insignificant, can ripple through time, shaping not only our lives but also those of future generations. The personal legacy we create is an amalgamation of our achievements, our failures, our love, and our regrets. It is the summation of our efforts to live a life of purpose and significance.

Emotional and Psychological Impact

BEYOND THE TANGIBLE marks we leave behind, there are the indelible emotional and psychological footprints we imprint on the hearts and minds of those around us. Our interactions, whether fleeting or enduring, have profound effects that can uplift or burden those we encounter.

This book also explores the depth of these emotional legacies. How do our words and actions affect others? What scars or blessings do we impart through our relationships? These are the questions that guide our journey into understanding the unseen impacts of our lives. Through personal anecdotes, psychological insights, and reflective narratives, we delve into the complexities of human connections and the enduring power of emotional influence.

Reflection and Hope

AS YOU READ, I INVITE you to pause and reflect on your own life's journey. Consider the legacy you are building, both in your personal achievements and in the hearts of those you touch. Think about the stories you want to be told about you and the emotions you wish to evoke in those who remember you.

In a world often preoccupied with material success and fleeting moments, "What We Leave Behind" calls us to a deeper contemplation of our true legacy. It encourages us to live with intention, to act with kindness, and to cherish the relationships that define our lives.

May this book be a companion in your reflections and an inspiration in your journey towards leaving a legacy that resonates with love, wisdom, and profound impact.

Chapter 1: Understanding Personal Legacy and Life Reflections

The Importance of Leaving a Lasting Impact

In our journey through life, we often get caught up in the day-to-day hustle and bustle, focusing on our own needs and desires. However, it is important to take a step back and consider the bigger picture - what kind of impact are we leaving on the world? The Legacy Blueprint: A Guide to Leaving a Lasting Impact on the World emphasizes the importance of leaving a lasting legacy that will outlive us and continue to inspire others long after we are gone.

Leaving a lasting impact is not just about achieving fame or fortune, but about making a positive difference in the lives of others. It is about leaving behind a legacy that reflects our values, beliefs, and passions, and inspires future generations to do the same. By focusing on leaving a lasting impact, we can find meaning and purpose in our lives, and create a sense of fulfillment that transcends our own existence.

For many of us, the thought of our own mortality can be daunting and anxiety-provoking. However, by embracing the idea of leaving a lasting impact, we can find peace and comfort in knowing that our lives have meaning and significance. This can help us cope with our mortality anxiety and find solace in the knowledge that our legacy will continue to live on, even after we are gone.

In the end, leaving a lasting impact is about more than just making a name for yourself - it is about creating a legacy that reflects the essence of who you are and what you stand for. By focusing on leaving a positive mark on the world, you can find peace, fulfillment, and meaning in your own life, and inspire others to do the same. The Legacy Blueprint is a guide to help you on this journey, and empower you to leave a lasting impact that will endure long after you are gone.

In the whirlwind of everyday life, it's easy to become absorbed in our immediate goals and responsibilities. However, there comes a time when we must pause and reflect on the broader implications of our actions and choices. What kind of mark are we leaving on the world? How will our contributions be remembered? These questions are at the heart of understanding the importance of leaving a lasting impact. This exploration delves into the essence of creating a legacy that not only transcends our individual existence but also inspires and enriches the lives of others for generations to come.

Understanding the Concept of Lasting Impact

LEAVING A LASTING IMPACT means contributing to the world in ways that endure beyond our lifetime. It is about making meaningful changes that resonate through time, influencing and benefiting others long after we are gone.

Defining Legacy

LEGACY IS MORE THAN just a collection of achievements or accolades. It is the enduring influence we leave on the lives of others and the world around us.

- **Personal Contributions**: Consider how your actions and decisions have shaped your environment and the lives of those you touch. Legacy is built through these personal contributions, big and small, that collectively define your impact.

- **Values and Principles**: Reflect on the values and principles that guide your actions. A lasting legacy is often rooted in these core beliefs, which inspire and direct your efforts towards meaningful goals.

Enduring Influence

THE TRUE MEASURE OF a lasting impact is the enduring influence it has on others. This influence can manifest in various forms, from inspiring change in individual lives to contributing to societal advancements.

- **Inspiring Others**: Think about how your life and work inspire others. Do your actions encourage others to pursue their passions, live authentically, or contribute positively to their communities?

• **Sustainable Change**: Focus on creating changes that are sustainable and continue to provide benefits long after they are initiated. This could involve mentoring, creating innovative solutions, or supporting initiatives that have a lasting impact.

Finding Meaning and Purpose Through Impact

THE PURSUIT OF LEAVING a lasting impact is deeply intertwined with finding meaning and purpose in life. By striving to make a positive difference, we can discover a sense of fulfillment that transcends our personal existence.

Aligning Actions with Purpose

ALIGNING YOUR ACTIONS with your sense of purpose ensures that your efforts are meaningful and contribute to a legacy that reflects your true self.

• **Identifying Your Purpose**: Take time to explore what gives your life meaning. What passions drive you? What causes resonate with your values? Identifying your purpose helps guide your efforts towards creating a lasting impact.

- **Living Purposefully**: Make conscious choices that align with your purpose. Whether through your career, volunteer work, or personal relationships, living purposefully amplifies your impact and ensures it reflects your authentic self.

Creating Fulfillment Through Contribution

CONTRIBUTING TO THE well-being of others and the world can bring profound fulfillment. It connects us to something larger than ourselves and gives our lives a deeper sense of significance.

- **Acts of Service**: Engage in acts of service that benefit others. Whether it's helping a neighbor, volunteering in your community, or supporting a cause, these actions contribute to a legacy of compassion and generosity.

- **Building Positive Relationships**: Foster positive relationships that uplift and support those around you. The impact you have on others' lives through kindness, encouragement, and empathy is a cornerstone of a lasting legacy.

Embracing Legacy as a Motivational Force

THE CONCEPT OF LEGACY can serve as a powerful motivational force, encouraging us to live with intention and to strive for excellence in our endeavors.

Overcoming Challenges

THE DESIRE TO LEAVE a lasting impact can inspire us to overcome challenges and persist in the face of adversity. It provides a sense of direction and resilience, motivating us to keep going even when the path is difficult.

- **Resilience in Adversity**: Let the vision of your legacy inspire you to persevere through tough times. The challenges you face are often the crucibles that forge your greatest contributions.

- **Dedication to Growth**: Commit to continuous growth and improvement. By striving to better yourself and your efforts, you increase the potential for your legacy to have a lasting, positive impact.

Inspiring Excellence

STRIVING TO LEAVE A lasting legacy encourages us to pursue excellence in all that we do. It prompts us to seek out opportunities for growth, to innovate, and to make meaningful contributions in our chosen fields.

- **Pursuing Excellence**: Aim for excellence in your endeavors. Whether in your professional work, creative projects, or personal relationships, the pursuit of excellence amplifies your impact and sets a high standard for those who follow.

- **Innovative Contributions**: Look for ways to innovate and make unique contributions. Your creativity and ingenuity can lead to breakthroughs that have a significant and enduring impact.

Reflecting on Mortality and Embracing Legacy

CONTEMPLATING OUR MORTALITY can bring a heightened awareness of the importance of our legacy. It can shift our focus from transient goals to lasting contributions that endure beyond our lifetime.

Legacy as a Comfort in Mortality

THE AWARENESS OF OUR finite existence can be daunting, but it can also provide comfort in knowing that our actions can continue to make a difference even after we are gone.

- **Finding Peace in Legacy**: Embrace the idea that your legacy will live on through the lives you touch and the contributions you make. This realization can bring a sense of peace and fulfillment.

- **Focus on Lasting Impact**: Prioritize actions and goals that have the potential for long- term impact. By focusing on what endures, you can find solace in the knowledge that your influence will persist.

Living with Intentionality

UNDERSTANDING THE SIGNIFICANCE of legacy encourages us to live with intentionality. It inspires us to make choices that align with our values and to act in ways that contribute to our desired impact.

- **Intentional Living**: Make deliberate choices that reflect your values and aspirations. Living with intentionality ensures that your actions are purposeful and aligned with your vision of a lasting legacy.

• **Mindful Presence**: Cultivate a mindful presence in your daily life. Being fully present in each moment allows you to engage deeply and to make meaningful contributions in all areas of your life.

Crafting a Legacy Blueprint

CREATING A LEGACY BLUEPRINT involves defining the impact you want to have and developing a plan to achieve it. This blueprint serves as a guide for living a life that reflects your values and aspirations.

Defining Your Impact

START BY DEFINING THE specific impact you want to have. Consider the areas of your life where you can make a meaningful contribution and the legacy you want to leave behind.

• **Identifying Key Areas**: Identify the key areas where you want to make a difference. This could be in your personal relationships, professional work, or community involvement.

- **Setting Goals**: Set clear, achievable goals that align with your vision of a lasting impact. These goals provide direction and motivation, guiding your efforts towards meaningful contributions.

Developing a Plan

ONCE YOU'VE DEFINED your impact, develop a plan to achieve it. This plan should include actionable steps and strategies for making a positive difference.

- **Actionable Steps**: Break down your goals into actionable steps. These steps should be specific and attainable, providing a roadmap for creating your desired impact.

- **Strategic Planning**: Develop strategies for overcoming obstacles and maximizing your impact. Consider how you can leverage your strengths and resources to achieve your goals.

The importance of leaving a lasting impact extends far beyond personal achievement. It is about making meaningful contributions that resonate through time, enriching the lives of others and the world around us. By understanding the concept of legacy, finding fulfillment through contribution, and embracing the motivational force of our desired impact, we can create a legacy that reflects our true selves and inspires future generations.

Evelyn's Story: A Journey of Legacy and Reflection

AS I SIT BY THE WINDOW of my cozy little apartment, watching the city I've called home for over forty years, I find myself reflecting on my life. At 75, I have a lot of memories, many beautiful moments, and some tough ones too. The hum of the city below feels like a distant echo of the hustle and bustle that once filled my days. Now, with my children grown and my career behind me, I often think about what I've left behind and the legacy I hope to pass on.

I was born and raised in a modest neighborhood in Atlanta. My parents, a teacher and a factory worker, taught me the values of hard work and the importance of education. They always told me I could achieve anything if I set my mind to it. As a young girl, I dreamed big and worked hard in school, hoping to make my mark on the world.

I was fortunate to earn a scholarship to a prestigious university, where I pursued a degree in environmental science. From a young age, I was passionate about the environment. I remember spending countless hours outdoors, fascinated by the beauty of nature and concerned about how we were treating our planet. This passion led me to a career as an environmental activist, where I dedicated myself to fighting climate change and promoting sustainability.

In my thirties, I married James, my college sweetheart, and we started a family. We had two wonderful children, Marcus and Lila. Balancing my career with raising a family was no easy task, but I was determined to be both a devoted mother and a dedicated advocate for the environment. I often took Marcus and Lila to rallies and events, teaching them the importance of standing up for their beliefs and making a positive difference in the world.

Over the years, I saw the fruits of my labor. Our community became more environmentally conscious—cleaner parks, better recycling programs, and a growing awareness about the importance of protecting our planet. It was incredibly rewarding to see these changes and to know that my efforts were making a difference. But more than the public recognition and the visible results, what fulfilled me most was the sense of purpose I found in my work.

Everything changed in my sixties when James passed away suddenly from a heart attack. Losing him was the hardest thing I've ever faced. It forced me to confront my own mortality and question whether my life's work had truly made a lasting impact. I wondered, was I leaving behind something meaningful? Would my efforts continue to inspire others long after I was gone?

In my search for answers, I turned to legacy coaching. It was through this process that I began to explore my values, passions, and goals on a much deeper level. My coach encouraged me to journal about my experiences and to meditate on what truly mattered to me. Through these practices, I started to see my life as part of a larger story—one that extended beyond my own existence.

Legacy coaching helped me recognize the quiet, yet profound, ways I had touched the lives of others. I realized that my legacy wasn't just in the environmental changes I had championed but also in the values I had passed on to my children and the many people I had inspired along the way.

One project that became particularly dear to my heart was the community garden I helped establish in our neighborhood. It started as a small plot of land but grew into a vibrant space where families came together to grow their own food, connect with nature, and learn about sustainable living. Seeing how this garden brought people together and fostered a sense of community filled me with immense joy and pride.

Even now, I continue to nurture this garden, sharing my knowledge and passion with the younger generations. I love sitting with the neighborhood children, teaching them about the importance of caring for the earth and for each other. These moments are precious to me—they are my living legacy, a testament to the values I hold dear and the impact I hope to leave behind.

As I watch the sun set over the city, I feel a deep sense of peace and fulfillment. I know that my legacy is not measured by fame or fortune but by the positive differences I have made in the lives of others. My journey has taught me that leaving a lasting impact is about more than personal success; it's about creating ripples of change that continue to inspire and uplift others long after we are gone.

Looking back, I see that my life's journey has been a rich tapestry of moments, each contributing to the legacy I leave behind. From my early days dreaming big in Atlanta, to my career as an environmental activist, to the family I've cherished and the community garden I've nurtured, every step has been part of a larger story.

I hope my story inspires others to reflect on their own lives and the impact they want to leave on the world. Each of us has the potential to create a legacy that transcends our own existence, one that enriches the lives of others and fosters a better, more compassionate world. Through our values, passions, and actions, we can all leave behind a legacy that truly matters.

So, as I continue to embrace the wisdom of my later years, I hold onto the belief that our legacies are the stories we write through our lives, the values we live by, and the love and inspiration we share with those around us. This is the legacy I strive to leave behind—a legacy of purpose, passion, and positive change.

Reflecting on Your Life Journey

AS WE JOURNEY THROUGH life, it is important to take the time to reflect on our experiences, choices, and accomplishments. Reflecting on our life journey allows us to gain insight into who we are, where we have been, and where we are headed. It is a powerful tool for personal growth and self- discovery.

In the book "The Legacy Blueprint: A Guide to Leaving a Lasting Impact on the World," we delve into the importance of reflecting on your life journey. By taking the time to reflect on your past experiences, you can gain a deeper understanding of yourself and your purpose in life. This self-reflection can help you identify your strengths and weaknesses, as well as your values and beliefs.

Reflecting on your life journey also allows you to consider what kind of legacy you want to leave behind. What impact do you want to have on the world? What do you want to be remembered for? By thinking about these questions, you can begin to shape your legacy and make a lasting impact on those around you.

Through reflective practices such as journaling, meditation, and mindfulness, you can cultivate gratitude and meaning in your life. These practices can help you appreciate the present moment, find peace in the face of death, and cope with mortality anxiety. By exploring spirituality and existential questions in relation to your personal legacy, you can gain a deeper understanding of your place in the world and the impact you want to have.

If you are seeking to leave a lasting impact on the world, consider working with a legacy coach who can guide you in reflecting on your life journey and shaping your legacy. Together, you can explore your values, beliefs, and goals, and create a plan for leaving a meaningful impact on the world. Remember, your legacy is not just what you leave behind when you are gone – it is the impact you make on the world during your lifetime. Reflect on your life journey, cultivate gratitude and meaning, and leave a lasting impact on the world.

As we traverse the path of life, it's crucial to pause and reflect on the journey we have undertaken. Life, with its myriad experiences and choices, shapes who we are and the legacy we wish to leave behind. Reflection is not just a nostalgic review of the past; it is a profound tool for personal growth and self-discovery. It offers us the opportunity to understand our true selves, acknowledge our accomplishments, and envision the impact we want to have on the world.

The Power of Reflection

IN "THE LEGACY BLUEPRINT: A Guide to Leaving a Lasting Impact on the World," the importance of reflecting on your life journey is emphasized as a key component of creating a meaningful legacy. Reflection allows us to step back from the whirlwind of daily life and consider the broader narrative of our existence. By doing so, we gain insights into our strengths and weaknesses, our values and beliefs, and our purpose and direction in life.

Through reflection, we can:

1. **Understand Ourselves Better**: Examining our experiences helps us identify patterns in our behavior and decisions, giving us a clearer understanding of who we are and what drives us.
2. **Acknowledge Our Growth**: Reflecting on our past challenges and successes allows us to appreciate how far we have come and the personal growth we have achieved.
3. **Shape Our Future**: By understanding our past and present, we can make more informed and intentional decisions about our future, aligning our actions with our deepest values and aspirations.

Shaping Your Legacy

REFLECTION IS A POWERFUL tool for shaping the legacy you wish to leave behind. It prompts us to ask fundamental questions about our lives: What impact do we want to have on the world? What do we want to be remembered for? These questions help us define our legacy and guide our actions toward making a lasting and meaningful impact.

To shape your legacy, consider the following steps:

1. **Identify Your Core Values**: Reflect on what matters most to

you. What principles and beliefs guide your actions? Your legacy should be a reflection of these core values.

2. **Envision Your Desired Impact**: Think about the mark you want to leave on the world. How do you want to be remembered by those who know you and by future generations?

3. **Align Your Actions with Your Legacy**: Once you have a clear vision of your legacy, take steps to align your daily actions and long-term goals with this vision. This ensures that your legacy is not just an end goal but a guiding force throughout your life.

Reflective Practices

INCORPORATING REFLECTIVE practices into your routine can significantly enhance your understanding of yourself and your legacy. Here are a few practices that can help:

1. **Journaling**: Writing about your thoughts, experiences, and feelings can provide clarity and insight. It allows you to explore your inner world and track your personal growth over time.

1. **Meditation and Mindfulness**: These practices help you stay present and cultivate a deeper awareness of your thoughts and emotions. They can also provide a sense of peace and perspective, especially when dealing with existential questions.
2. **Gratitude Exercises**: Reflecting on what you are grateful for can foster a positive outlook and help you appreciate the richness of your life experiences.

Coping with Mortality and Embracing Spirituality

REFLECTION OFTEN LEADS us to confront existential questions about life and death. While these questions can be daunting, they also offer an opportunity for profound insight and peace. By exploring spirituality and our relationship with mortality, we can gain a deeper understanding of our place in the world and find solace in the legacy we are creating.

1. **Finding Peace in Mortality**: Embracing the reality of our mortality can help us appreciate the present moment and find peace in the knowledge that our lives have meaning and significance.
2. **Exploring Spirituality**: Whether through religious practices, philosophical inquiry, or a connection with nature, exploring spirituality can provide a sense of purpose and belonging that enriches our understanding of our legacy.

A Pathway to Purpose

1. **Clarify Your Vision**: Gain a clearer understanding of the legacy you want to create and how to align your actions with this vision.
2. **Set Meaningful Goals**: Identify specific, actionable steps

that will help you achieve your desired impact.

3. **Cultivate Purpose and Fulfillment**: Find deeper meaning and satisfaction in your life by living in accordance with your legacy.

Living Your Legacy

ULTIMATELY, YOUR LEGACY is not just about what you leave behind when you are gone; it is the impact you make on the world throughout your lifetime. By reflecting on your life journey, cultivating gratitude and meaning, and taking intentional actions, you can create a legacy that truly reflects who you are and what you stand for.

As you continue on your journey, remember that every moment is an opportunity to shape your legacy. Reflect on your experiences, embrace your values, and strive to make a positive difference in the lives of others. In doing so, you will leave a lasting impact that resonates far beyond your time on this earth.

Identifying Your Values and Beliefs

IN ORDER TO LEAVE A lasting impact on the world, it is crucial to first identify your values and beliefs. Your values are the guiding principles that shape your behavior and decisions, while your beliefs are the deeply held convictions that influence your perspective on life. By understanding what you truly value and believe in, you can create a legacy that is authentic and meaningful.

Take some time to reflect on what matters most to you. What do you stand for? What principles do you hold dear? By identifying your core values, you can align your actions with your beliefs, leading to a more purposeful and fulfilling life. Your values are the essence of who you are, and they will ultimately shape the legacy you leave behind.

It is also important to examine your beliefs and attitudes towards life. What do you believe about the world and your place in it? Are there any limiting beliefs that are holding you back from reaching your full potential? By exploring your beliefs, you can uncover any unconscious biases or negative thought patterns that may be hindering your personal growth.

Exploring spirituality and existential questions in relation to your personal legacy can also bring depth and meaning to your life. What do you believe happens after death? How do you define spirituality and connection to something greater than yourself? By delving into these existential questions, you can gain a deeper understanding of your purpose and the impact you want to make in the world.

By identifying your values and beliefs, you can create a legacy that reflects your true essence and leaves a lasting impact on the world. By aligning your actions with your values, exploring your beliefs and spirituality, and reflecting on your personal legacy, you can cultivate gratitude, meaning, and peace in your life. Remember, your legacy is not just what you leave behind, but the impact you make on the world while you are here.

Discovering My Legacy: James' Journey of Values and Beliefs

AS I SIT ON THE PORCH of my home in the quiet countryside, I find myself reflecting on the journey that has brought me here. My name is James, and at 68, I'm still uncovering the layers of my own life story. The past few years have been a time of profound introspection, as I search for the values and beliefs that have shaped my desire to leave a positive legacy. This journey of self- discovery has been both challenging and rewarding, revealing the essence of who I am and what I stand for.

I grew up in a small town in Ohio, where my parents ran a local grocery store. They were hardworking, honest people who instilled in me a strong work ethic and a sense of responsibility. But as a young man, I was restless and eager to find my own path. After high school, I moved to the city to attend college, fueled by a desire to escape the predictability of small-town life and discover what the world had to offer.

In those early years, I was driven by ambition and a desire to make something of myself. I pursued a career in finance, believing that success was measured by the size of your paycheck and the prestige of your job title. For a while, I was caught up in the fast-paced world of corporate finance, working long hours and chasing promotions. But deep down, I felt a nagging sense of emptiness. I began to question the values that were driving me and whether they truly reflected who I was.

It wasn't until my mid-forties that I started to seriously question my path. The catalyst was a conversation with my father, who was in declining health. We were sitting on the porch of my childhood home, much like I am now, and he asked me a simple but profound question: "What do you want to be remembered for?" His words struck a chord deep within me. I realized that I had been living according to values that weren't my own, chasing a definition of success that felt hollow.

That conversation was a turning point. It prompted me to embark on a journey of self-discovery, to understand what I truly valued and believed in. I took a step back from my career and began to reflect on what mattered most to me. What principles did I hold dear? What kind of impact did I want to have on the world?

Through introspection and conversations with loved ones, I started to uncover my core values. I realized that honesty, compassion, and community were central to who I am. I wanted my life to be guided by these principles, to be someone who made a positive difference in the lives of others.

One of the most significant steps in this journey was leaving my corporate job and starting a community project in my neighborhood. I used my financial skills to help set up a local cooperative that provided affordable housing and resources for low-income families. It was a labor of love, aligning my actions with my values and bringing a deep sense of fulfillment that I had never felt in the corporate world.

Identifying my values was just one part of the journey. I also needed to examine my beliefs about life and my place in the world. I started to explore spirituality, something I had never given much thought to before. I read books on various philosophies and religions, attended workshops, and spent time in nature, seeking to understand my connection to something greater than myself.

One of the most challenging aspects was confronting my beliefs about mortality. The death of my father had left me grappling with questions about what happens after we die and the legacy we leave behind. I found solace in the idea that our impact on the world continues through the lives we touch and the values we instill in others.

During this period of reflection, I also became aware of certain limiting beliefs that had been holding me back. I realized that I had often measured my worth by external achievements rather than my inner character and contributions. This mindset had kept me from pursuing paths that truly resonated with my values.

By acknowledging and challenging these beliefs, I began to see that my worth was not tied to my job title or income, but to the positive impact I made in my community and the love I shared with those around me. This shift in perspective was liberating, allowing me to embrace a more authentic and fulfilling life.

Now, as I sit on this porch, I am at peace with the journey I have undertaken. My legacy is not defined by financial success or professional accolades, but by the values I live by and the impact I have on the lives of others. I am proud of the community project I helped build, the relationships I have nurtured, and the principles that guide my life.

Reflecting on my values and beliefs has been a journey of profound self-discovery. It has helped me align my actions with my true self and create a legacy that I am proud of. I have learned that our legacy is not just what we leave behind when we are gone, but the positive impact we make on the world while we are here.

As I move forward, I continue to reflect on my life journey, cultivating gratitude for the experiences that have shaped me and the opportunities to make a difference. I strive to live each day in alignment with my values, knowing that every moment is an opportunity to leave a positive mark on the world.

My story is still unfolding, and I am grateful for the chance to continue discovering, growing, and contributing. By embracing my values and beliefs, I hope to leave a legacy that reflects the essence of who I am and inspires others to do the same.

Creating Your Legacy Blueprint

IN THE JOURNEY OF LIFE, we all have the opportunity to leave behind a legacy that will continue to impact the world long after we are gone. This is a powerful and meaningful way to make our mark on the world and ensure that our presence is felt for generations to come. Creating your legacy blueprint is a way to map out how you want to be remembered and the impact you want to have on the world.

When creating your legacy blueprint, it is important to start by reflecting on your values, beliefs, and the things that are most important to you. What do you want your legacy to say about who you are as a person? What kind of impact do you want to have on the world? These are important questions to consider as you begin the process of creating your legacy blueprint.

One key aspect of creating your legacy blueprint is reflecting on your life and the experiences that have shaped you into the person you are today. What lessons have you learned along the way? What challenges have you overcome? By reflecting on your life experiences, you can gain a deeper understanding of who you are and what you want your legacy to be.

Another important step in creating your legacy blueprint is exploring your spirituality and existential questions in relation to your personal legacy. What do you believe happens after we die? How does your spirituality shape the way you want to be remembered? By exploring these deep questions, you can gain a greater sense of clarity and purpose in creating your legacy blueprint.

As you create your legacy blueprint, it is also important to address any fears or anxieties you may have about mortality and death. By confronting these fears head-on, you can find peace and acceptance in the face of death, allowing you to focus on living a life that is meaningful and fulfilling. Legacy coaching can be a powerful tool in helping you navigate these emotions and find peace in the face of death.

Creating a legacy blueprint is a deeply personal and transformative journey. It's about defining how you want to be remembered and the impact you want to have on the world. For me, this journey began with a period of introspection and reflection, allowing me to align my life's actions with my core values and beliefs. Let me share with you how I went about creating my own legacy blueprint, and how you can embark on this fulfilling journey yourself.

Starting with Reflection

TO CREATE YOUR LEGACY blueprint, start by looking inward. Reflect on your values and beliefs—the guiding principles that define who you are. Ask yourself what you stand for and what kind of person you want to be remembered as. For me, the process began with quiet evenings on my porch, reflecting on the experiences that shaped me and the lessons I learned from them.

1. **Identify Your Core Values**: Write down the values that are most important to you. For me, honesty, compassion, and community were at the top of the list. These values became the foundation of my legacy blueprint.

2. **Reflect on Life Experiences**: Consider the significant moments and challenges in your life. How have they shaped your character and values? I thought about my father's advice, my years in corporate finance, and the fulfillment I found in community service. These reflections helped me understand what truly mattered to me.

3. **Define Your Desired Impact**: Envision the impact you want to have on the world. How do you want to be remembered by your family, friends, and community? I wanted my legacy to be about making a positive difference in the lives of others, particularly through supporting sustainable and compassionate initiatives.

Exploring Spirituality and Existential Questions

PART OF CREATING A legacy blueprint involves exploring your spirituality and grappling with existential questions. These reflections provide depth and purpose to your legacy.

1. **Consider What Happens After Death**: Your beliefs about the afterlife can influence how you approach your legacy. I found peace in the idea that my actions and values would live on through the people and projects I touched.

2. **Define Your Spiritual Connection**: Reflect on your spiritual beliefs and how they guide your actions. Whether through religious faith, philosophical inquiry, or a connection with nature, spirituality can offer a profound sense of purpose. For me, spending time in nature and helping others brought me closer to understanding my place in the world.

3. **Contemplate Your Purpose**: Ask yourself what gives your life meaning. Understanding your purpose can help you create a legacy that is both fulfilling and impactful. My purpose, I realized, was to foster community and support sustainable living.

Addressing Fears and Anxieties About Mortality

CREATING A LEGACY BLUEPRINT also means confronting any fears or anxieties about death and mortality. It's natural to have concerns about the end of life, but facing these fears can lead to peace and acceptance.

1. **Acknowledge Your Fears**: Write down any fears or anxieties you have about death. For a long time, I was afraid of not having enough time to make a difference. Acknowledging this fear helped me focus on what I could do each day to live in alignment with my values.

2. **Seek Peace and Acceptance**: Find ways to cultivate peace with the idea of mortality. This might involve meditation, counseling, or spiritual practices. For me, talking to a legacy coach helped immensely. They guided me through my fears and helped me find acceptance and purpose.

3. **Focus on the Present**: While planning for the future is important, living in the present allows you to appreciate the journey. Embrace each moment as an opportunity to live out your values and contribute to your legacy. I learned to value my daily interactions and the small, positive actions I could take every day.

Crafting Your Legacy Blueprint

WITH THESE REFLECTIONS and insights, you're ready to start crafting your legacy blueprint. This blueprint is a map of how you want to be remembered and the steps you'll take to create that legacy.

1. **Set Clear Goals**: Define specific goals that align with your values and desired impact. For example, my goals included expanding the community garden project and mentoring

young professionals in sustainable business practices.

2. **Create a Plan of Action**: Outline the actions you'll take to achieve your goals. Break them down into manageable steps. For my community project, this involved securing funding, recruiting volunteers, and setting up educational workshops.

3. **Stay Flexible and Open**: Your legacy blueprint is a living document. Be open to revisiting and revising it as you grow and your circumstances change. I regularly review my blueprint to ensure it still aligns with my evolving values and life experiences.

Embracing Reflective Practices

TO SUPPORT YOUR JOURNEY, incorporate reflective practices and consider working with a legacy coach.

1. **Journaling**: Regularly writing about your thoughts and experiences can provide clarity and keep you connected to your values and goals. My journal became a trusted companion, helping me track my progress and reflect on my journey.
2. **Meditation and Mindfulness**: These practices help you stay present and cultivate a deeper connection with your values. They've been instrumental in helping me find peace and purpose in my daily life.

Living Your Legacy

REMEMBER, YOUR LEGACY is not just about what you leave behind—it's about the impact you make while you are here. Each day is an opportunity to live in alignment with your values and contribute to your legacy. By creating and following your legacy blueprint, you ensure that your life reflects your true essence and leaves a lasting, positive impact on the world.

In conclusion, creating your legacy blueprint is a powerful way to leave a lasting impact on the world and ensure that your presence is felt for generations to come. By reflecting on your values, beliefs, life experiences, and spirituality, you can create a legacy that is meaningful and purposeful. Through reflective practices and legacy coaching, you can cultivate gratitude and meaning in your life, leaving behind a legacy that will continue to inspire and impact others long after you are gone.

Chapter 2: Emotional Well-being and Fundamental Human Concerns

Navigating Emotions Surrounding Legacy

Navigating emotions surrounding legacy can be a complex and deeply personal journey. Our legacy is not just about what we leave behind for others, but also about how we come to terms with our own mortality and the impact we have had on the world. It is a reflection of our values, beliefs, and the relationships we have cultivated throughout our lives.

As we explore our personal legacy and life reflections, it is important to acknowledge and embrace the full spectrum of emotions that come with it. From feelings of pride and accomplishment to moments of regret and sorrow, each emotion plays a vital role in shaping our understanding of our legacy. By allowing ourselves to fully experience and process these emotions, we can gain a deeper sense of meaning and purpose in our lives.

In the process of navigating emotions surrounding legacy, we may also find ourselves grappling with existential questions and exploring our spirituality. These questions can be both daunting and enlightening, pushing us to confront our beliefs and values in a profound way. By delving into these deeper aspects of ourselves, we can begin to uncover the true essence of our legacy and the impact we wish to leave on the world.

Coping with mortality anxiety and finding peace in the face of death is an essential part of the legacy-building process. By accepting our own mortality and embracing the impermanence of life, we can begin to live more fully in the present moment. This acceptance can also serve as a powerful motivator to create a legacy that aligns with our values and aspirations, inspiring us to make the most of our time on this earth. By engaging in reflective practices and cultivating gratitude and meaning in life, we can truly leave a lasting impact on the world and create a legacy that will endure for generations to come.

As I sit here reflecting on my journey of creating a legacy, I am reminded of the vast array of emotions that accompany this process. Legacy is not just about the tangible impact we leave behind; it's deeply intertwined with our emotions, values, and the way we reconcile with our own mortality. The journey of understanding and building our legacy is rich with emotional experiences—moments of pride, fulfillment, regret, and even sorrow.

For me, the pride and sense of accomplishment come from seeing the positive changes in my community and the lives I've touched through my work. There's a deep satisfaction in knowing that my efforts have made a difference, however small. Whether it's the flourishing community garden I helped establish or the young professionals I've mentored, these achievements remind me that I've contributed something meaningful to the world.

But along with pride, there are also feelings of regret and sorrow. I think about the opportunities I missed or the times I acted out of alignment with my values. These reflections can be painful, but they are also invaluable. They offer a chance to learn and grow, to acknowledge our imperfections, and to strive for better in the future. Accepting these moments as part of our journey allows us to build a more authentic and honest legacy.

As we delve into the emotions surrounding our legacy, we inevitably encounter existential questions. These questions challenge us to examine our beliefs about life, death, and our place in the world. For me, this exploration has been both daunting and enlightening.

Spiritual Exploration

EXPLORING MY SPIRITUALITY has been a significant part of understanding my legacy. Whether through quiet moments in nature, meditative practices, or philosophical readings, I've sought to understand my connection to something greater than myself. This exploration has brought a sense of peace and purpose, guiding me to live in a way that aligns with my deepest values and beliefs.

Grappling with Mortality

COPING WITH THE REALITY of my mortality has been one of the most profound aspects of this journey. Accepting that our time on earth is finite can be a difficult but transformative realization. It has pushed me to live more fully in the present and to focus on what truly matters. The awareness of my mortality has also been a powerful motivator to create a legacy that reflects my values and aspirations.

Coming to terms with death and embracing the impermanence of life is crucial in the legacy- building process. By accepting our mortality, we can shift our focus from fear to the richness of living in the present moment. This acceptance fosters a deeper appreciation for life and drives us to make the most of our time here.

Learning to live fully in the present has been a key part of finding peace. It's about savoring the simple moments, nurturing relationships, and engaging in activities that bring joy and fulfillment. This approach has helped me appreciate the journey rather than just the destination, enriching my daily life and contributing to a meaningful legacy.

The acceptance of death as a natural part of life has also motivated me to be intentional about my legacy. It has inspired me to focus on actions and decisions that align with my values, knowing that each moment contributes to the lasting impact I want to leave. This process has been instrumental in helping me align my life with my legacy aspirations.

Engaging in reflective practices has been a cornerstone of my legacy-building journey. These practices include journaling, meditation, and cultivating gratitude.

Regular journaling has provided a space to process my thoughts and emotions. It's allowed me to track my progress, reflect on my experiences, and stay connected to my values and goals.

Journaling has become a vital tool for maintaining clarity and focus on my legacy journey.

Meditation and mindfulness practices have helped me stay present and cultivate a deeper awareness of my thoughts and feelings. They've been essential in finding peace with my mortality and staying aligned with my values.

Practicing gratitude has enriched my life by helping me appreciate the abundance around me. It's shifted my focus from what's missing to what's meaningful, fostering a sense of fulfillment and purpose that's integral to my legacy.

In conclusion, navigating the emotions surrounding legacy is a deeply personal and enriching journey. It involves embracing a full spectrum of emotions, confronting existential questions, and finding peace with our mortality. Legacy coaching and reflective practices can guide us in creating a legacy that truly reflects our values and aspirations.

Dealing with Regrets and Forgiveness

DEALING WITH REGRETS and forgiveness is an essential part of leaving a lasting legacy on the world. In order to truly make a positive impact, we must first come to terms with our past mistakes and learn to forgive ourselves and others. It is only through this process that we can move forward with clarity, purpose, and a sense of inner peace.

Regrets can weigh heavily on our minds and hearts, holding us back from reaching our full potential and leaving a meaningful legacy. It is important to acknowledge these regrets, but also to recognize that dwelling on them does not serve us in any way. Instead, we must learn from our mistakes, make amends where possible, and then release them with forgiveness and compassion.

Forgiveness is a powerful tool that can help us let go of the past and create space for new beginnings. By forgiving ourselves and others, we free ourselves from the burden of resentment and anger, allowing us to move forward with a renewed sense of purpose and clarity. It is through forgiveness that we can truly heal and create a legacy that is built on love, compassion, and understanding.

In order to cultivate forgiveness and let go of regrets, it is important to practice self-reflection and self-awareness. This may involve journaling, meditation, therapy, or other reflective practices that help us explore our thoughts and emotions in a safe and supportive way. By delving deep into our inner world, we can gain a better understanding of ourselves and come to terms with our past actions.

As we navigate the journey of leaving a lasting impact on the world, it is important to remember that we are all human and prone to making mistakes. By embracing forgiveness and letting go of regrets, we can pave the way for a legacy that is rooted in love, compassion, and understanding. May we all find the strength and courage to forgive ourselves and others, and create a legacy that will inspire and uplift future generations.

Sarah's Journey Through Regrets and Redemption

AS I SIT IN MY FAVORITE corner of the living room, with the soft glow of the evening sun streaming through the windows, I find myself deep in reflection. I'm Sarah, in my mid-30s, and life has brought me to a place where the past and present often intertwine, weaving a complex tapestry of memories, regrets, and hard-won forgiveness. The journey to this moment has been filled with challenges, mistakes, and the profound realization that forgiveness is not just an act but a pathway to inner peace and clarity.

My young adult years were marked by a series of decisions and actions that, looking back, fill me with a mix of regret and longing for a do-over. I was 22 when I moved to the city, eager to carve out a life on my own terms. The excitement of newfound independence and the pursuit of career dreams often overshadowed the quieter, more meaningful aspects of life.

In my twenties, I was driven by ambition and the need to prove myself. I worked long hours, climbing the corporate ladder, and often placed my career above relationships. I remember missing countless family gatherings, neglecting friendships, and even ending a relationship with someone who genuinely cared for me because I believed my career came first.

One of the most searing memories from my past is the day I let my younger sister, Emma, down in a way that would haunt me forever. Emma, vibrant and full of dreams, had always looked up to me. She often called me her hero, the one she wanted to emulate as she carved out her own path in life. Her college graduation was a milestone she had worked tirelessly to achieve, and my promise to be there by her side meant everything to her.

I can still recall the excitement in her voice when she told me about the ceremony. "I can't wait to see you there, Sarah," she had said. "It won't be the same without you." But when the day came, a last-minute work crisis demanded my attention. In the cold, sterile light of my office, I made the decision to stay, convincing myself that this was just another sacrifice in the name of ambition.

When I called Emma to break the news, her voice was filled with a quiet disbelief. "But you promised," she whispered, as if trying to hold back the tears. I could hear the crack in her voice, the pain and disappointment. It was a sound that pierced through me, deeper than any criticism or setback I had ever faced.

I hung up the phone, staring blankly at my computer screen, but the weight of that moment settled heavily on my shoulders. The image of Emma standing in her graduation gown, looking out into the crowd for a sister who never arrived, burned into my memory. It was a scene I would never witness, a moment forever lost.

Months later, Emma was involved in a tragic accident, and I never got the chance to make amends. The news shattered me. The last memory she had of me was a broken promise, and the last image I carried of her was a face filled with unspoken pain. That day at the office, I lost more than just time with my sister; I lost the chance to be there in one of her proudest moments, and the opportunity to tell her how much she meant to me.

The regret from that day has become a silent companion in my life, a poignant reminder of the choices I made and the time that slipped through my fingers. It's a sorrow that will always linger, urging me to live more fully, to be more present, and to never again let the pressures of the moment overshadow the people who matter most.

The weight of her loose and these regrets grew heavier as I entered my thirties. I began to realize that the pursuit of success had come at the expense of the people who mattered most. The turning point came during a quiet evening much like this one. I was sorting through old photographs when I came across a picture of Emma and me, taken years before that missed graduation. Her smile was bright and full of admiration, and I was struck by how much I had let her down.

It was then that I knew I needed to change. I couldn't rewrite the past, but I could seek forgiveness and, more importantly, learn to forgive myself. Forgiving myself wasn't easy. It required deep introspection and a commitment to understanding the person I had been and the person I wanted to become. I turned to journaling, writing down my thoughts and feelings as a way to process my regrets and the emotions they stirred up. Through these entries, I began to see patterns in my behavior and understand the underlying fears and insecurities that had driven my choices.

Meditation also became a sanctuary for me. Each morning, I would sit quietly, focusing on my breath, and allowing the thoughts of regret and self-reproach to pass through my mind without judgment. This practice helped me cultivate a sense of peace and acceptance, acknowledging that while I had made mistakes, they didn't define who I was. I was more than my past actions.

Therapy played a crucial role in my healing journey as well. With the guidance of a compassionate therapist, I explored my emotions and confronted the fears that had led me to prioritize work over relationships. We worked on developing self-compassion, helping me to see myself not as a flawed individual but as someone capable of growth and change.

As I continue to navigate daily life, the lessons of forgiveness and self-compassion have become integral to my approach. I've learned to balance my career ambitions with the importance of nurturing relationships. I make time for family and friends, understanding that these connections are the true foundation of a meaningful life.

At work, I've become more mindful of the impact my actions have on others. I strive to lead with empathy and to create a supportive environment for my colleagues. The drive for success has been replaced with a desire to contribute positively to the lives of those around me.

As I reflect on my journey, I see that dealing with regrets and finding forgiveness have been crucial steps in creating a legacy rooted in love, compassion, and understanding. My past mistakes no longer hold me back; instead, they have become lessons that guide me toward a more fulfilling and purposeful life.

I want my legacy to be one of kindness and connection, where my actions reflect the values I hold dear. I hope to inspire others to forgive themselves and to embrace the beauty of second chances. We are all human, capable of making mistakes, but also capable of profound growth and transformation.

In this journey of life, dealing with regrets and embracing forgiveness are essential parts of leaving a lasting impact on the world. It is through acknowledging our mistakes, seeking forgiveness, and learning to forgive ourselves that we pave the way for a legacy built on love and compassion.

As I continue to navigate the challenges of daily life, I carry with me the lessons of forgiveness and the commitment to live in alignment with my true values. Each day is an opportunity to create a positive impact, to nurture relationships, and to build a legacy that will inspire and uplift future generations. May we all find the strength and courage to forgive ourselves and others, and to create a legacy that reflects the best of who we are.

Finding Purpose and Meaning in Life

FINDING PURPOSE AND meaning in life is a fundamental human concern that has been pondered for centuries by philosophers, psychologists, and individuals seeking to leave a lasting impact on the world. In the journey of creating our personal legacy, it is essential to explore our innermost desires and values to uncover what truly gives our lives meaning and fulfillment. By reflecting on our past experiences, relationships, and accomplishments, we can gain insight into what brings us joy and purpose.

When we take the time to delve deep into our emotions and beliefs, we may discover that our legacy is not just about the tangible achievements we leave behind, but also the intangible qualities that define who we are as individuals. It is through exploring spirituality and existential questions that we can connect with a deeper sense of purpose and meaning that transcends our physical existence. By embracing our mortality and acknowledging the impermanence of life, we can find peace in the face of death and live each day with gratitude and intention.

Throughout human history, the search for purpose and meaning has been a central theme in our quest for a fulfilling life. This profound journey isn't just a philosophical inquiry but a deeply personal and transformative process. To understand what gives our lives true significance, we must delve into the depths of our desires, aspirations, and the experiences that shape us. It's a path that invites us to look inward, explore the richness of our inner world, and discover what makes life genuinely meaningful.

The Journey Within

FINDING PURPOSE BEGINS with an inward journey—a careful examination of the thoughts, feelings, and motivations that drive us. This self-exploration helps us understand what gives us a sense of fulfillment and guides our actions in a way that resonates with our true selves.

Reflect on the moments that have brought you the deepest joy and satisfaction. These are often the clearest indicators of what you value most. For some, it might be the quiet satisfaction of a job well done, while for others, it could be the joy found in creative expression or helping others.

Look at the underlying motivations behind your choices and actions. What compels you to get up each morning? What pursuits make you lose track of time? These motivations are key to uncovering your intrinsic purpose.

Each person's journey to finding meaning is unique, shaped by individual experiences and personal insights. This uniqueness is what makes our contributions to the world so valuable. Consider the significant milestones and turning points in your life. How have these events shaped your perspective and priorities? The insights gained from these reflections can illuminate the path to a life of purpose.

The challenges and adversities we face often play a crucial role in defining our purpose. They teach resilience, provide opportunities for growth, and help us discover strengths we didn't know we had. Living a life of meaning involves more than introspection; it requires intentional action and a commitment to align our daily lives with our deeper values. Identify the goals that resonate most with your sense of purpose. These goals should reflect what you find genuinely rewarding and be aligned with your vision of a fulfilling life.

Immerse yourself in activities that ignite your passion. Whether it's through your work, hobbies, or community involvement, engaging with what you love brings a profound sense of fulfillment. The connections we form with others are integral to a meaningful life. These relationships enrich our experiences and provide a foundation for shared purpose and mutual support. Foster relationships that are deep and authentic. These connections bring joy and provide a sense of belonging, helping to shape a life filled with meaning. Consider how you can positively impact the lives of those around you. Acts of kindness, support, and mentorship not only enhance their lives but also add a layer of purpose to yours.

Finding purpose also involves looking beyond our immediate concerns and considering our place in the larger scheme of things. Recognize how your actions and choices ripple out into the world. Understanding this interconnectedness can guide you to make decisions that contribute positively to the broader community and environment. Cultivate a sense of inner peace through practices that align with your sense of purpose. This could involve mindfulness, contemplation, or simply spending time in nature.

Living with Intention

A MEANINGFUL LIFE IS characterized by living with intention and clarity. It's about making conscious choices that reflect our values and purpose.

Practicing Mindful Decision-Making

APPROACH EACH DECISION with mindfulness, ensuring that your actions align with your deeper sense of purpose. This mindful approach fosters a life that feels coherent and fulfilling.

Celebrating Small Wins

ACKNOWLEDGE AND CELEBRATE the small victories along your journey. Each step taken towards a life of purpose is a significant achievement that contributes to your overall sense of fulfillment.

The quest for purpose and meaning is a deeply personal journey that calls us to explore the essence of who we are and what we value. It's about understanding the joys and motivations that drive us, embracing the challenges that shape us, and crafting a life that resonates with our true selves.

As we navigate this journey, it's essential to build meaningful relationships, engage passionately with life, and consider our impact on the broader world. By living with intention and celebrating each step towards our purpose, we create a life rich with significance and fulfillment.

May we each find the courage to embark on this journey of discovery, to live authentically, and to pursue a life of profound meaning and purpose.

Embracing Change and Uncertainty

EMBRACING CHANGE AND uncertainty is a fundamental aspect of our journey towards leaving a lasting impact on the world. In the face of life's unpredictability, it is essential to cultivate a mindset of resilience and adaptability. Instead of resisting change, we must learn to embrace it as an opportunity for growth and transformation. By allowing ourselves to flow with the currents of change, we open ourselves up to new possibilities and experiences that can enrich our lives and deepen our impact on the world.

Uncertainty can be a source of fear and anxiety for many of us, especially when it comes to facing the unknowns of our own mortality. However, by leaning into uncertainty with courage and curiosity, we can discover a sense of freedom and liberation. Embracing the impermanence of life can lead us to a deeper appreciation for the present moment and a greater sense of gratitude for the time we have on this earth. By acknowledging the uncertainty of our existence, we can find a newfound sense of purpose and meaning in our lives.

Exploring spirituality and existential questions in relation to our personal legacy can provide us with a deeper understanding of our place in the universe. By connecting with something greater than ourselves, whether it be through religion, nature, or meditation, we can find solace in the face of life's uncertainties. By delving into the fundamental human concerns of existence and legacy, we can gain a clearer perspective on what truly matters in life and how we can make a meaningful impact on the world.

Coping with mortality anxiety and finding peace in the face of death is a journey that requires courage and introspection. By acknowledging our fears and anxieties surrounding death, we can begin to unravel the layers of existential dread that may be holding us back from living fully in the present moment. By embracing our mortality as a natural part of life, we can find peace and acceptance in the face of death, allowing us to live more authentically and purposefully.

Change and uncertainty are constants in the ever-evolving journey of life. As we strive to leave a lasting impact, it becomes essential to embrace these elements with resilience and an open heart. Life's unpredictability, while challenging, also offers endless opportunities for growth, learning, and transformation. By accepting and navigating change, we can enrich our lives and deepen our contributions to the world.

The Nature of Change

CHANGE IS AN INEVITABLE part of life. It can come in various forms—new career opportunities, changes in relationships, or unexpected events. Each of these changes presents a chance to grow and adapt. Facing change requires a flexible mindset and the ability to adapt to new circumstances. Instead of resisting these transitions, we can learn to flow with them, using each as a stepping stone towards personal and collective growth.

• **Openness to Transformation**: Embrace the potential for transformation that change brings. Whether it's a new job, a move to a different city, or a shift in personal relationships, every change carries the seed of new opportunities.

• **Learning from Each Phase**: Each phase of life, whether filled with challenges or successes, offers valuable lessons. Reflecting on these can help us navigate future changes with more insight and confidence.

The Power of Adaptability

ADAPTABILITY IS A CRUCIAL skill in handling change. It allows us to respond effectively to new situations and to thrive in environments of uncertainty.

• **Flexibility in Action**: Being adaptable means being willing to change our plans and approaches when necessary. This flexibility enables us to make the most of evolving situations.

• **Resilience in the Face of Challenges**: Building resilience helps us withstand the pressures of change. It strengthens our ability to bounce back from setbacks and continue moving forward with purpose.

Uncertainty can be daunting, often accompanied by feelings of anxiety and fear. However, embracing uncertainty can open doors to unexpected and enriching experiences. Approaching uncertainty with curiosity turns potential anxiety into a journey of exploration and discovery. It encourages us to view the unknown as an opportunity rather than a threat.

- **Curiosity as a Compass**: Let curiosity guide you through uncertain times. By asking questions and exploring new possibilities, you can uncover paths that lead to personal and professional growth.

- **Openness to New Experiences**: Embrace new experiences and perspectives that come your way. Each one has the potential to expand your understanding and enrich your life.

- **Living Without Rigid Plans**: While having goals is important, being too rigid can limit our ability to respond to change. Embracing uncertainty means allowing room for spontaneity and flexibility in our plans.

- **Freedom to Experiment**: Uncertainty provides the freedom to experiment and try new things. This openness to experimentation can lead to innovation and creativity in both personal and professional spheres.

The Role of Resilience

RESILIENCE IS THE ABILITY to recover from setbacks and continue pursuing our goals despite challenges. It is a vital trait for navigating change and uncertainty. Resilience is built through experiences and the development of inner strength. It involves cultivating a mindset that sees challenges as opportunities for growth.

• **Cultivating a Positive Outlook**: Focus on the positive aspects of change and the potential for growth. A positive outlook can help you maintain motivation and energy even in the face of difficulties.

• **Developing Coping Strategies**: Learn and practice strategies to cope with stress and setbacks. These might include mindfulness techniques, physical exercise, or seeking support from friends and family.

• **Commitment to Goals**: Stay focused on your long-term goals, even when faced with obstacles. This commitment provides a sense of direction and purpose.

• **Learning from Setbacks**: View setbacks as learning opportunities. Each challenge offers insights that can help you improve and adapt in the future.

Creating a Lasting Impact

IN THE FACE OF CHANGE and uncertainty, creating a lasting impact requires a clear vision and the ability to adapt as circumstances evolve. A clear vision helps guide your actions and decisions, providing a sense of direction amidst the flux of change.

• **Articulating Your Goals**: Clearly define what you want to achieve and the impact you wish to make. This clarity will help you stay focused and motivated.

• **Aligning Actions with Vision**: Ensure that your actions align with your vision. This alignment will help you navigate changes and maintain a consistent path towards your goals.

• **Strategic Flexibility**: Build flexibility into your plans. This allows you to adjust your strategies in response to new challenges and opportunities.

• **Continuous Learning**: Commit to continuous learning and growth. Stay open to new ideas and be willing to adapt your approach based on new insights and experiences.

Fostering Meaningful Connections

RELATIONSHIPS PLAY a crucial role in how we navigate change and uncertainty. Building strong, supportive connections can provide stability and perspective. Invest in relationships that offer mutual support and understanding. These connections can provide a foundation of stability in times of change. Engaging with your community and contributing to the well-being of others can enhance your sense of purpose and provide a broader perspective.

• **Nurturing Supportive Networks**: Build and maintain networks of supportive relationships. These can include family, friends, mentors, and colleagues who can offer guidance and encouragement.

• **Communicating Openly**: Foster open and honest communication within your relationships. Clear communication helps build trust and allows for mutual support during challenging times.

• **Volunteering and Service**: Get involved in activities that contribute to your community. Volunteering and service provide a sense of connection and purpose.

- **Sharing Knowledge and Skills**: Share your knowledge and skills with others. This not only helps those around you but also reinforces your own sense of purpose and impact.

Living with Intention

EMBRACING CHANGE AND uncertainty involves living with intention and clarity. It means making conscious choices that reflect your values and goals. Mindfulness helps us stay present and aware, allowing us to navigate change with grace and resilience. Acknowledge and celebrate your progress, no matter how small. Each step forward is a testament to your resilience and adaptability.

- **Being Present in the Moment**: Practice mindfulness to stay focused on the present moment. This awareness helps you respond to change with calmness and clarity.

- **Reflecting on Actions**: Regularly reflect on your actions and decisions. Consider how they align with your goals and whether they are helping you navigate change effectively.

- **Recognizing Achievements**: Take time to recognize and celebrate your achievements. This reinforces your motivation and encourages continued growth.

- **Learning from Successes and Failures**: Reflect on both your successes and failures. Each provides valuable lessons that can help you navigate future changes more effectively.

Embracing change and uncertainty is essential for creating a meaningful and lasting impact. By developing resilience, adapting to new circumstances, and staying open to new experiences, we can navigate the complexities of life with confidence and purpose.

As we move through life's journey, let us welcome change as an opportunity for growth and view uncertainty as a gateway to new possibilities. By living with intention, fostering meaningful connections, and maintaining a flexible approach, we can create a legacy that resonates with our true selves and inspires others.

Chapter 3: Exploring Spirituality and Existential Questions in Relation to Personal Legacy

Connecting with Your Spiritual Beliefs

In this subchapter, we will explore the importance of connecting with your spiritual beliefs as a key component of leaving a lasting impact on the world. Our spiritual beliefs are deeply personal and can provide us with a sense of purpose, meaning, and connection to something greater than ourselves. By tapping into our spiritual beliefs, we can find guidance, strength, and peace in our journey towards creating a meaningful legacy.

Connecting with your spiritual beliefs is a powerful way to cultivate a sense of gratitude and meaning in life. When we align our actions with our spiritual beliefs, we can experience a greater sense of fulfillment and purpose. By taking the time to reflect on our spiritual beliefs and integrate them into our daily lives, we can live with intention and create a legacy that reflects our deepest values and beliefs.

Exploring spirituality and existential questions in relation to personal legacy can help us confront our mortality anxiety and find peace in the face of death. By delving into the deeper questions of life and death, we can gain a greater understanding of our place in the world and the impact we want to leave behind. Through reflection and introspection, we can come to terms with our mortality and find solace in the knowledge that our legacy will live on beyond our physical existence.

Spiritual beliefs play a profound role in shaping our sense of purpose and guiding our actions. Whether rooted in organized religion, personal spirituality, or a deep connection to nature, these beliefs can provide us with a framework for understanding our place in the world and our relationship to something greater than ourselves. By connecting with our spiritual beliefs, we can find the strength, guidance, and peace necessary to leave a lasting impact on the world. This exploration delves into how integrating our spiritual beliefs into our daily lives can help us create a meaningful legacy that reflects our deepest values and aspirations.

The Power of Spiritual Connection

OUR SPIRITUAL BELIEFS offer a source of inner strength and guidance that can help us navigate life's challenges and uncertainties. They provide a deeper sense of purpose and help us understand our role in the larger tapestry of existence. Spiritual beliefs can be a wellspring of resilience, helping us find the courage to face difficult times and the wisdom to make meaningful choices. A strong connection to our spiritual beliefs can foster a profound sense of peace and fulfillment, enriching our daily lives and our interactions with others.

- **Inner Resilience**: Spirituality often provides a deep reservoir of strength that we can draw upon during challenging times. This resilience helps us maintain a sense of purpose and direction, even when faced with adversity.

- **Guiding Principles**: Spiritual beliefs offer guiding principles that can shape our decisions and actions. These principles help us navigate life's complexities with integrity and compassion.

- **Sense of Peace**: Spirituality can bring a sense of peace and calm, helping us to find balance and serenity amidst the chaos of everyday life.

- **Fulfillment through Alignment**: When our actions align with our spiritual beliefs, we experience a deeper sense of fulfillment and purpose. This alignment fosters a life that is coherent and meaningful.

Integrating Spiritual Beliefs into Daily Life

TO TRULY BENEFIT FROM our spiritual beliefs, we must integrate them into our daily lives. This involves reflecting on our beliefs, aligning our actions with our values, and finding ways to express our spirituality through our interactions and choices. Taking time to reflect on our spiritual beliefs helps us understand how they influence our actions and decisions. This introspection can deepen our connection to our beliefs and clarify our sense of purpose. Aligning our actions with our spiritual beliefs ensures that we live authentically and with integrity. This alignment is crucial for creating a legacy that truly reflects who we are. Expressing spirituality in our daily interactions and choices helps bring our beliefs to life. This expression can take many forms, from acts of kindness to participating in spiritual practices.

- **Daily Reflection**: Set aside time each day for quiet reflection on your spiritual beliefs. Consider how these beliefs shape your thoughts, actions, and interactions with others.

- **Journaling**: Writing about your spiritual journey can provide insights into your values and how they align with your actions. Journaling helps you articulate your beliefs and track your spiritual growth.

- **Consistency in Action**: Strive to ensure that your actions consistently reflect your spiritual values. This consistency fosters authenticity and helps build a legacy grounded in your true self.

- **Ethical Decision-Making**: Use your spiritual beliefs as a guide for making ethical decisions. Let these principles inform how you interact with others and how you contribute to your community.

- **Acts of Kindness**: Small acts of kindness and compassion can be powerful expressions of your spiritual beliefs. These actions contribute to a legacy of love and positive impact.

- **Participation in Spiritual Practices**: Engage in practices that reflect your spirituality, such as prayer, meditation, or community service. These practices reinforce your connection to your beliefs and provide opportunities to express them in tangible ways.

Exploring Existential Questions

DELVING INTO EXISTENTIAL questions about life, purpose, and our place in the universe can deepen our understanding of our spiritual beliefs and how they shape our legacy. Reflecting on the purpose of life and our role in the world helps us connect with our deeper motivations and aspirations. Exploring our place in the universe provides a broader perspective on our lives and our contributions. This understanding can inspire us to live more intentionally and leave a lasting legacy.

- **Meaningful Reflection**: Consider what gives your life meaning and how your spiritual beliefs influence this understanding. Reflect on how you can live in a way that aligns with these insights.

- **Purposeful Living**: Use your spiritual beliefs to guide your pursuit of purpose. Let them inform your goals and the ways in which you seek to make a positive impact on the world.

- **Interconnectedness**: Recognize the interconnectedness of all life and how your actions impact the larger world. This perspective fosters a sense of responsibility and inspires you to contribute positively to the collective well-being.

- **Legacy in Context**: Consider how your legacy fits into the larger context of human existence. Reflect on the ways in which your spiritual beliefs shape your vision of the impact you want to leave behind.

Connecting with your spiritual beliefs is a vital aspect of creating a meaningful and lasting legacy. By exploring and integrating these beliefs into your daily life, you can find strength, guidance, and fulfillment. Reflecting on existential questions and aligning your actions with your values allows you to live authentically and with purpose.

As you navigate your spiritual journey, consider embracing your spirituality, living with intention, and expressing your beliefs through your actions, you can create a legacy that truly reflects your deepest values and inspires others for generations to come.

Embracing Spirituality: Richard's Journey of Legacy and Meaning

I'M RICHARD, AND AS I sit here in the quiet countryside, reflecting on the path my life has taken, I'm struck by how much my spiritual journey has influenced my thoughts on legacy and the impact I want to leave behind. Growing up, I never gave much thought to spirituality. But as I've navigated the ups and downs of life, I've come to realize that connecting with something greater than myself has provided a profound sense of purpose and direction. This is the story of how spirituality reshaped my understanding of what truly matters and how I want to be remembered.

In my twenties, I was consumed by the typical markers of success—career advancement, financial stability, and social recognition. I worked tirelessly in the fast-paced world of corporate law, driven by a desire to climb the ladder and make a name for myself. Yet, despite my achievements, there was a lingering sense of emptiness, a feeling that something significant was missing.

I remember the turning point vividly. It was a cold, grey morning in December. I had just closed a major deal at work, one that should have brought a sense of triumph and celebration. Instead, as I looked out of my office window, I felt an overwhelming emptiness. The constant grind and the superficial rewards no longer satisfied me. It was as if I was living someone else's life, pursuing goals that didn't align with who I truly was.

That winter, seeking respite from the corporate chaos, I decided to take a week off and retreat to a cabin in the mountains. Alone with my thoughts, surrounded by the serene beauty of nature, I began to confront the questions that had been gnawing at me. What was my life's purpose? What did I truly value? And most importantly, how did I want to be remembered?

One morning, as I watched the sunrise over the snow-covered peaks, I felt a profound sense of peace and connection. It was as if the universe was gently nudging me to explore deeper, to find the answers within myself. This was the start of my spiritual journey.

Back in the city, I started exploring various spiritual practices. I attended meditation classes, read books on different philosophies, and even participated in a few silent retreats. These experiences were eye-opening, revealing aspects of myself that I had long ignored. Through meditation, I found a stillness and clarity that had eluded me for years. I began to understand that spirituality wasn't about adhering to a specific doctrine or belief system; it was about connecting with my inner self and the world around me in a meaningful way.

As I delved deeper into my spiritual practice, I noticed a shift in my relationships and daily interactions. I became more present and compassionate, less driven by ego and more by a genuine desire to connect with others. My conversations with friends and family took on new depth, and I found joy in the simple moments of life that I had previously overlooked.

One particularly transformative moment came during a family gathering. My younger brother, David, who I had always felt a bit disconnected from, opened up to me about his struggles with anxiety. In the past, I might have offered quick, pragmatic advice. But this time, I listened deeply and shared my own journey of finding peace through spirituality. It was a turning point in our relationship, and we've grown closer ever since.

As my spiritual journey unfolded, it began to reshape my thoughts on legacy. I realized that the impact I wanted to leave wasn't about the professional accolades or financial success I had once chased. Instead, it was about the intangible qualities I cultivated—kindness, empathy, and a deep connection with others.

I started to think about how I could contribute to the world in a way that aligned with my spiritual values. This led me to volunteer at a local community center, where I helped mentor young adults from disadvantaged backgrounds. Sharing my experiences and guiding them as they navigated their own challenges brought a sense of fulfillment that no corporate achievement ever had.

Living in alignment with my spiritual beliefs also meant embracing my authentic self. I began to make choices that reflected my true values rather than societal expectations. This included leaving my high-stress job to start a small legal consultancy focused on helping non-profits and social enterprises. It was a leap of faith, but it felt right. For the first time in years, I was living a life that resonated with my deepest values and desires.

I also made a conscious effort to simplify my life. I let go of the constant need for more—more money, more status, more possessions—and instead focused on what truly mattered: meaningful work, deep relationships, and a sense of peace and contentment.

Today, my spiritual journey is ongoing. It's a path of continuous learning and growth, one that challenges me to look within and to connect with the world in deeper, more meaningful ways. I'm not striving for perfection; rather, I'm embracing the journey, with all its ups and downs, as a way to live more authentically and purposefully.

When I think about my legacy now, it's no longer about what I've achieved but how I've lived. I want to be remembered as someone who was kind, who listened deeply, and who sought to make a positive difference in the lives of others. I want my legacy to reflect the values and beliefs that have become the foundation of my life.

Connecting with my spiritual beliefs has been a transformative journey, reshaping my understanding of purpose, legacy, and what it means to live a fulfilling life. It has taught me to value the intangible qualities that truly matter and to align my actions with my deepest values. As I continue on this path, I am committed to living each day with intention and authenticity, striving to leave behind a legacy that reflects the essence of who I am and the impact I want to make on the world.

Contemplating Existential Questions

IN THE DEPTHS OF OUR minds and souls, we are often faced with existential questions that stir our emotions and challenge our beliefs. These questions about the meaning of life, the purpose of our existence, and what happens after we are gone can leave us feeling overwhelmed and uncertain. However, it is through contemplation of these profound questions that we can truly discover our own personal legacy and leave a lasting impact on the world.

As we journey through life, it is important to take the time to reflect on our own existence and consider what we want to leave behind for future generations. By exploring our fundamental human concerns and contemplating the legacy we wish to create, we can begin to understand the true meaning of our lives and the impact we have on those around us. This process of self- reflection is essential for personal growth and emotional well-being.

In the end, it is through contemplation of existential questions and reflection on our own mortality that we can truly understand the legacy we wish to leave behind. By exploring spirituality, embracing impermanence, and cultivating gratitude and meaning in our lives, we can create a lasting impact on the world that transcends our own existence. Let us embrace the journey of self-discovery and leave a legacy that will inspire others to live with purpose and passion.

Finding Peace in the Present Moment

IN THE FAST-PACED WORLD we live in, it can be easy to get caught up in the chaos of everyday life. We often find ourselves worrying about the future or dwelling on the past, forgetting to appreciate the beauty and peace that can be found in the present moment. But what if we were to shift our focus and truly embrace the here and now?

In the stillness of our most private moments, we often encounter existential questions that reach into the very core of our being. These profound inquiries about the essence of life, our purpose in the grand scheme, and the legacy we will leave behind can be both unsettling and illuminating.

They compel us to step beyond the mundane and consider our place in the vast tapestry of existence. While these questions can evoke feelings of doubt and confusion, they also hold the key to unlocking a deeper understanding of ourselves and our journey through life.

Existential questions are those that transcend everyday concerns and touch upon the fundamental aspects of our human experience. They urge us to explore the deeper meanings and implications of our lives, often prompting us to reflect on the big picture and our role within it.

At some point, many of us find ourselves asking, "What is the meaning of my life?" This question goes beyond the pursuit of goals or the fulfillment of responsibilities. It asks us to consider the broader significance of our existence and the unique contribution we can make to the world. The profound nature of existential questions can often lead to feelings of overwhelm and uncertainty. These emotions are a natural response to confronting the vastness and complexity of life. However, learning to navigate these feelings can help us find clarity and direction. Confronting existential questions requires us to embrace vulnerability. It involves acknowledging our fears, doubts, and the limitations of our understanding.

- **Finding Personal Significance**: Discovering what gives our life meaning involves looking at our passions, values, and the causes we care about. It requires us to connect with what truly resonates within us and provides a sense of fulfillment.

• **Creating a Life of Purpose**: By identifying what brings meaning to our lives, we can create a path that aligns with our deepest aspirations. This journey towards purpose is often marked by a commitment to living authentically and making a positive impact.

• **Accepting Uncertainty**: Accepting that we may not have all the answers allows us to explore these questions with openness and curiosity. This acceptance can be liberating, freeing us from the pressure to find definitive solutions.

• **Finding Strength in Vulnerability**: Embracing vulnerability can be a source of strength. It allows us to connect more deeply with ourselves and others, fostering a sense of empathy and compassion in our relationships.

Cultivating a Reflective Mindset

DEVELOPING A REFLECTIVE mindset helps us engage with existential questions in a thoughtful and meaningful way. This approach encourages us to consider our experiences, beliefs, and aspirations from a broader perspective. Engaging with existential questions can be a transformative process. It invites us to reevaluate our priorities, redefine our goals, and discover a sense of purpose that aligns with our true selves. Contemplating the deeper aspects of life often leads us to reassess our priorities. It encourages us to focus on what truly matters and to let go of pursuits that no longer serve our growth and fulfillment. Existential contemplation challenges us to rethink traditional notions of success. It prompts us to define success in terms of personal fulfillment and the positive impact we have on others, rather than external achievements or material wealth.

- **Making Time for Reflection**: Set aside regular time for reflection. Whether through journaling, meditation, or quiet contemplation, these moments of introspection can provide valuable insights into our deeper questions.

- **Seeking Diverse Perspectives**: Engage with different viewpoints and philosophies. This exploration can enrich our understanding and help us see our own questions in a new light.

- **Focusing on What Matters Most**: Identify the aspects of life that are most important to you. This might include relationships, personal growth, or contributions to your community. Prioritizing these elements can lead to a more meaningful and satisfying life.

- **Letting Go of the Unnecessary**: Be willing to release activities or goals that do not align with your core values. This process of letting go creates space for more purposeful endeavors.

- **Aligning Success with Values**: Redefine success in a way that aligns with your values and aspirations. Consider how your achievements contribute to your sense of purpose and the well-being of those around you.

- **Celebrating Personal Growth**: Recognize and celebrate your personal growth and the progress you make in your journey towards meaning. These milestones are a testament to your commitment to living a purposeful life.

Creating a Personal Legacy Through Existential Inquiry

ONE OF THE MOST PROFOUND outcomes of engaging with existential questions is the insight they provide into the legacy we wish to leave behind. This legacy is a reflection of our values, beliefs, and the impact we hope to have on the world. Defining your legacy involves considering the lasting contributions you want to make and how you want to be remembered. This process is deeply personal and evolves over time as you gain clarity and understanding. Your legacy is not only about the present but also about how it will resonate with future generations. Consider how your actions and contributions can inspire and support those who come after you. Incorporating existential contemplation into our daily lives can enrich our experiences and deepen our understanding of ourselves and the world around us. Cultivate mindful awareness in your daily activities. This practice encourages you to stay present and connected to the deeper questions that shape your life. Commit to continuous learning and personal growth. This journey involves exploring new ideas, challenging your beliefs, and remaining open to change.

- **Articulating Your Impact**: Reflect on the ways you want to contribute to the world. What difference do you want to make? How do you want your actions to be remembered by others?

- **Living Your Legacy Today**: Start living your legacy now. Align your daily actions with the impact you want to create and the values you wish to embody.

- **Inspiring Others**: Think about how you can inspire others through your journey and the insights you have gained. Share your experiences and wisdom to encourage others to explore their own existential questions.

• **Supporting Long-Term Impact**: Focus on initiatives and actions that have a lasting effect. Whether through mentorship, community involvement, or personal relationships, seek ways to create a positive impact that endures.

• **Practicing Mindfulness**: Engage in mindfulness practices that help you stay present and aware. This could include meditation, mindful walking, or simply taking a few moments each day to focus on your breath and surroundings.

• **Reflecting on Daily Experiences**: Use your daily experiences as opportunities for reflection. Consider how each moment contributes to your understanding of life and your sense of purpose.

• **Embracing Lifelong Learning**: Seek out new knowledge and experiences that expand your perspective. This continuous learning fosters personal growth and deepens your engagement with existential questions.

• **Welcoming Change and Evolution**: Be open to evolving your beliefs and understanding. As you grow and change, so too will your answers to the deeper questions of life.

Contemplating existential questions is a profound and transformative journey that invites us to explore the essence of our existence and the legacy we wish to create. By embracing these questions with curiosity and openness, we can navigate the complexities of life with greater clarity and purpose.

As we reflect on the deeper meanings of our lives, let us prioritize what truly matters, redefine our notions of success, and live each day in a way that aligns with our values and aspirations. Through this journey, we can create a legacy that reflects our true selves and leaves a lasting impact on the world.

May we all find the courage to engage with the profound questions that shape our existence and to build a life that is rich with meaning and purpose.

Understanding the Interconnectedness of All Beings

UNDERSTANDING THE INTERCONNECTEDNESS of all beings is a fundamental aspect of leaving a lasting impact on the world. In order to truly make a difference in the lives of others and leave a legacy that will endure long after we are gone, we must recognize the inherent connections that exist between all living creatures. When we understand that we are all part of a larger, interconnected web of life, we can begin to see the ripple effects of our actions and how they can impact not only ourselves, but those around us as well.

By embracing the interconnectedness of all beings, we can cultivate a deeper sense of empathy and compassion for others. When we recognize that we are all connected in some way, it becomes easier to see the humanity in others and treat them with kindness and respect. This understanding can lead to more meaningful relationships and a greater sense of fulfillment in our lives.

Exploring the interconnectedness of all beings can also help us cope with mortality anxiety and find peace in the face of death. When we understand that we are all part of a larger whole, we can come to terms with the impermanence of life and find solace in the knowledge that our actions can have a lasting impact on the world long after we are gone. This realization can bring a sense of peace and acceptance, allowing us to live more fully in the present moment.

As I reflect on my life's journey, I am continually drawn to the profound realization that we are all intricately connected. This understanding of interconnectedness has not only shaped my actions and relationships but also profoundly influenced my sense of purpose and the legacy I wish to leave behind. The awareness that every being is part of a larger, interconnected web of life has deepened my empathy, guided my choices, and brought a sense of peace and acceptance in the face of life's inevitable changes. This narrative explores how embracing the interconnectedness of all beings can transform our lives and help us leave a meaningful and enduring legacy.

My journey towards understanding interconnectedness began during a challenging period in my life. I had just moved to a new city for work, leaving behind friends and family. The sense of isolation was overwhelming, and I found myself questioning the purpose of my hurried, disconnected lifestyle. In search of solace, I started spending weekends hiking in the nearby mountains, where the beauty and complexity of nature began to reveal deeper truths about life.

One crisp autumn morning, as I sat by a serene lake surrounded by towering pines, I watched the gentle ripples on the water's surface. A single leaf had fallen, causing waves that radiated outwards, touching everything in their path. In that moment, it struck me how even the smallest actions could create waves that extend far beyond their point of origin. I realized that my life, too, was like that leaf; every choice I made, every action I took, had the potential to ripple out and affect others in ways I could never fully comprehend.

With this newfound awareness, I began to see the world through a different lens. Understanding that we are all part of a larger whole, I felt a growing sense of empathy and compassion for those around me.

This shift in perspective changed how I interacted with others and how I approached my personal and professional life.

At work, I started taking more time to listen to my colleagues, recognizing that their experiences and emotions were intertwined with mine. I realized that fostering a supportive and collaborative environment not only benefited the team but also enriched my own life. Simple acts of kindness, like offering a word of encouragement or lending a helping hand, created positive ripples that strengthened our collective spirit and productivity.

Outside of work, I became more engaged in my community. Volunteering at local shelters and participating in neighborhood clean-up efforts allowed me to connect with people from all walks of life. These experiences deepened my understanding of the diverse threads that make up our societal fabric and reinforced the importance of compassion and solidarity.

The Ripple Effect of Actions

AS I CONTINUED TO EXPLORE the concept of interconnectedness, I became increasingly aware of the ripple effects of my actions. This understanding compelled me to consider the broader impact of my choices and to strive to make decisions that contributed positively to the world around me.

Understanding our interconnectedness prompted me to adopt more sustainable and ethical practices in my daily life. I began to think more critically about the products I consumed, the companies I supported, and the environmental impact of my lifestyle. Choosing to reduce waste, support local businesses, and advocate for environmentally-friendly policies were small but significant ways to contribute to the well-being of the planet and its inhabitants.

Recognizing that my actions could inspire others, I sought to be a role model in both my personal and professional spheres. At work, I introduced initiatives focused on sustainability and community engagement. These efforts not only aligned with my values but also encouraged my colleagues to consider the broader impact of their actions. Seeing others adopt similar practices was a powerful reminder of how interconnected we all are and how each of us can contribute to positive change.

The understanding of interconnectedness also brought a profound sense of peace and acceptance, particularly in grappling with the uncertainties of life and the inevitability of death.

Coming to terms with the impermanence of life, I found comfort in the idea that our actions, no matter how small, could create lasting ripples in the world. This realization helped me cope with mortality anxiety and brought a sense of peace knowing that my contributions could continue to influence others long after I am gone.

Embracing interconnectedness encouraged me to live more fully in the present moment. I became more mindful of my interactions and more appreciative of the beauty in everyday experiences. Each moment, each connection, became an opportunity to contribute positively to the larger tapestry of life.

As I reflect on the legacy I want to leave behind, I am guided by the principle of interconnectedness. My goal is to create a legacy that reflects the values of empathy, compassion, and collective well-being.

I aim to foster a sense of community and collaboration in all aspects of my life. By bringing people together, whether through professional projects, community initiatives, or personal relationships, I hope to create an environment where everyone feels valued and supported. This legacy of connection is one that I believe will endure and inspire future generations.

I am also committed to supporting causes that extend beyond my immediate sphere. Whether through charitable donations, advocacy, or volunteer work, I strive to contribute to efforts that address larger societal and environmental issues. This broader perspective ensures that my legacy is not just about personal achievements but about making a meaningful impact on the world.

Understanding the interconnectedness of all beings has transformed my perspective on life and legacy. It has deepened my empathy, guided my actions, and brought a sense of peace and purpose to my journey. As I continue to navigate life's complexities, I am committed to living in a way that reflects our profound connection to each other and to the world around us.

By embracing the interconnectedness of life, we can cultivate meaningful relationships, make choices that benefit the greater good, and create legacies that inspire and uplift. May we all recognize the delicate web that binds us and strive to contribute positively to the beautiful, intricate tapestry of existence.

Chapter 4: Coping with Mortality Anxiety and Finding Peace in the Face of Death

Confronting Fear of Death

Confronting the fear of death is a fundamental human concern that often brings up feelings of anxiety, uncertainty, and even dread. However, coming to terms with our mortality is an essential part of leaving a lasting impact on the world. In order to truly live a purposeful life, we must first confront our fear of death and find peace in the face of the inevitable.

One way to confront the fear of death is to explore our personal legacy and life reflections. By reflecting on the impact we want to leave behind, we can begin to see death as a natural part of the cycle of life. When we focus on what we want to be remembered for, we can find meaning and purpose in our lives, even in the face of death.

Another important aspect of confronting the fear of death is exploring spirituality and existential questions. By delving into our beliefs about the afterlife, the meaning of life, and our place in the universe, we can gain a deeper understanding of death and find comfort in the unknown. By connecting with our spiritual beliefs, we can find peace in the face of mortality anxiety.

In the end, confronting the fear of death is a necessary step in leaving a lasting impact on the world. By exploring our personal legacy, delving into existential questions, and working with a legacy coach, we can find peace in the face of mortality anxiety and live a purposeful life.

Remember, death is not the end, but rather a new beginning in our journey towards leaving a lasting impact on the world.

Finding Peace and Defining Legacy: Jane and Mark's Story

JANE AND MARK HAD BUILT a life together over the span of forty years, weathering life's storms and celebrating its joys with unwavering love and companionship. Their journey was marked by shared dreams, deep bonds, and an unbreakable partnership. But as they faced profound losses— Jane coping with Mark's sudden passing and Mark confronting a life-threatening illness before his death—they were forced to reflect on their legacy, both as a couple and as individuals. This is their story of enduring love, loss, and the legacy they left behind.

Jane and Mark met in their twenties at a community event in their small hometown. Jane was a budding teacher with a passion for nurturing young minds, while Mark was an engineer who loved solving problems and creating innovative solutions. Their connection was immediate, and they quickly became inseparable, building a life together filled with mutual respect, love, and shared aspirations.

They were each other's steadfast support system, balancing Jane's nurturing and empathetic nature with Mark's analytical and steady approach to life. Together, they navigated the challenges of building careers, raising two daughters, and creating a home that was always open and welcoming.

Their lives took an unexpected turn on a bright spring morning. Mark had gone out for his routine bike ride, a cherished time he used to clear his mind and stay active. When he didn't return at the expected time, Jane's concern grew into dread. Hours later, she received the devastating news that Mark had suffered a fatal heart attack on the trail. He was gone, just like that, leaving Jane to face an unimaginable void.

Jane was shattered. The sudden loss of Mark, her partner and best friend, left her grappling with overwhelming grief and a sense of profound emptiness. As she struggled to cope with his absence, Jane found solace in reflecting on the life they had built together and the legacy of their shared journey.

In the solitude of her mourning, Jane began to contemplate the legacy they had created as a couple. Their life together had been marked by quiet, meaningful contributions rather than grand gestures, and it was these small acts of love and kindness that defined their legacy.

Jane thought about the home they had built, a sanctuary of love, laughter, and support. Their home had always been a gathering place for family and friends, a space where everyone felt welcome and valued. She cherished memories of family gatherings filled with warmth and joy— weekend barbecues, holiday celebrations, and late-night talks that strengthened their family's bonds. These moments were the essence of their shared life, fostering deep connections that would endure through the generations. Jane also reflected on their engagement with the community. Together, they had volunteered at local food banks, participated in neighborhood clean-ups, and supported educational programs. These efforts, though often unremarkable in their day-to-day lives, had left a lasting impact on those around them.

In the last years of his life, Mark faced a battle with a serious illness. The diagnosis was a shock, and the journey was fraught with challenges. Despite the gravity of his condition, Mark approached his illness with courage and a determination to make the most of his remaining time. Jane stood by Mark's side, providing unwavering support and care. They faced the illness together, finding strength in their love and in the shared moments of connection and understanding. Mark's courage in the face of his illness inspired everyone around him. He continued to work on his projects, mentor young engineers, and spend quality time with his family, all while battling the relentless progression of his disease. Jane and Mark made a conscious effort to cherish every moment. They traveled to places they had always wanted to see, shared long conversations about life and their hopes for the future, and deepened their connection with each passing day.

As Mark's condition worsened, he and Jane spent many hours reflecting on their life together and the legacy they wanted to leave behind. These conversations were a source of comfort and clarity, helping them to define the values and contributions that would continue to resonate after they were gone. They wanted their legacy to be one of love, learning, and lasting impact—values they had lived by throughout their marriage. They hoped their daughters would carry forward the love and support they had experienced at home, fostering strong, compassionate relationships in their own lives. Mark's passion for engineering and Jane's dedication to teaching were central to their identities. They decided to establish a scholarship fund for students pursuing careers in education and engineering, ensuring that their commitment to learning and innovation would continue to inspire future generations.

After Mark's passing, Jane found herself navigating life alone for the first time in decades. The grief was immense, but the legacy they had built together provided her with a sense of purpose and direction. Jane immersed herself in their shared projects, particularly the scholarship fund, which became a significant focus of her efforts. Through this work, she felt connected to Mark and the values they had cherished. She took great pride in seeing the scholarship fund grow and hearing from the students whose lives were touched by their support. Each success story was a testament to the lasting impact of their legacy. Jane continued their tradition of community involvement, volunteering and supporting local causes. These activities not only honored Mark's memory but also helped her find meaning and fulfillment in her new chapter of life.

Over time, Jane found a sense of peace bend acceptance. She came to understand that while Mark was no longer physically with her, his spirit and their shared values would always be a part of her life. Jane learned to embrace the present moment, finding joy in everyday experiences and connections. She nurtured her relationships with family and friends, appreciating the beauty of the life she had built. Living their legacy became Jane's way of keeping Mark's memory alive.

She took comfort in knowing that their love and contributions would continue to inspire and support others, creating a lasting impact that would endure through the years.

Jane and Mark's story is a testament to the enduring power of love, resilience, and shared values. Through the profound challenges of loss and illness, they found strength in each other and defined a legacy that reflected their deepest beliefs and aspirations.

As Jane continues her journey, she carries forward the lessons and values they cultivated together, leaving a legacy that honors their life as a couple and her individual path. Their story reminds us that even in the face of profound loss, we can find peace and purpose by focusing on the lasting impact of our lives and the love we share with others.

May we all find the courage to live our lives with intention, to cherish our connections, and to create legacies that inspire and uplift those who come after us.

Embracing Impermanence and Acceptance

IN THE JOURNEY OF LEAVING a lasting impact on the world, it is essential to embrace impermanence and acceptance. Life is constantly changing, and nothing lasts forever. By acknowledging the impermanence of all things, we can learn to let go of attachments and find peace in the present moment. Embracing impermanence allows us to appreciate the beauty of each passing moment and cherish the connections we have with others.

Acceptance is key to finding peace and fulfillment in life. When we accept the inevitability of change and impermanence, we can release the need for control and surrender to the flow of life. Acceptance does not mean resignation, but rather a willingness to face reality with courage and grace. By accepting our circumstances and ourselves as we are, we can cultivate a sense of inner peace and resilience in the face of adversity.

As we reflect on our personal legacy and life reflections, it is important to consider the fundamental human concerns that remain when we are gone. What impact do we want to leave behind? How do we want to be remembered by future generations? These questions can guide us in creating a meaningful legacy that reflects our values and beliefs. By exploring spirituality and existential questions in relation to our personal legacy, we can deepen our understanding of our purpose and significance in the world.

Coping with mortality anxiety and finding peace in the face of death is a profound challenge that many of us face. By embracing impermanence and acceptance, we can confront our fears of death and find peace in the knowledge that life is finite. Legacy coaching can provide support and guidance for individuals seeking to leave a lasting impact on the world. Through reflective practices that cultivate gratitude and meaning in life, we can create a legacy that reflects our unique gifts and contributions to the world.

In the end, embracing impermanence and acceptance is a transformative journey that can lead us to a deeper sense of fulfillment and purpose. By letting go of attachments and surrendering to the flow of life, we can find peace in the present moment and leave a legacy that will endure long after we are gone. Let us embrace impermanence and acceptance with open hearts and minds, knowing that our legacy is a reflection of our true essence and the impact we have on the world.

Cultivating a Sense of Peace and Serenity

IN THE HUSTLE AND BUSTLE of our daily lives, it can be easy to get caught up in the chaos and lose sight of what truly matters. However, cultivating a sense of peace and serenity is essential for our emotional well-being and overall happiness. In this subchapter, we will explore how we can tap into our inner peace and create a sense of tranquility that will not only benefit ourselves but also leave a lasting impact on the world.

One of the first steps in cultivating a sense of peace and serenity is to practice mindfulness. By being present in the moment and fully engaging with our surroundings, we can let go of worries about the past or future and focus on the beauty of the present. Mindfulness allows us to connect with our inner selves and find a sense of calm amidst the chaos of everyday life.

Another powerful tool for cultivating peace and serenity is the practice of gratitude. By taking time each day to reflect on the things we are grateful for, we can shift our focus from what we lack to what we have. Gratitude has the power to transform our perspective and bring a sense of contentment and peace into our lives.

In addition to mindfulness and gratitude, exploring spirituality can also be a powerful way to cultivate a sense of peace and serenity. Whether through prayer, meditation, or connecting with nature, spirituality can help us find a deeper sense of meaning and purpose in our lives. By tapping into our spiritual beliefs, we can find comfort and solace in the face of life's uncertainties.

Ultimately, cultivating a sense of peace and serenity is not just about benefiting ourselves, but also about leaving a lasting impact on the world. By embracing peace within ourselves, we can radiate that peace outwards and inspire others to do the same. As we embark on our journey of personal growth and self-discovery, let us remember that true peace comes from within and has the power to transform not only our own lives but the lives of those around us.

Creating a Legacy that Transcends Death

CREATING A LEGACY THAT transcends death is a powerful way to leave a lasting impact on the world and ensure that your influence continues long after you are gone. In the realm of psychology, self-help, and personal growth, understanding the importance of legacy and how to create one that truly resonates with others is key to living a fulfilling and meaningful life. When we reflect on our personal legacy and life reflections, we can begin to see the fundamental human concerns that drive us and shape our actions.

Exploring spirituality and existential questions in relation to our personal legacy can help us connect with something greater than ourselves and find deeper meaning in our lives. By grappling with our mortality anxiety and finding peace in the face of death, we can approach our legacy-building with a sense of purpose and clarity. Legacy coaching can be a valuable tool for individuals seeking guidance on how to leave a lasting impact on the world and make a difference in the lives of others.

Reflective practices, such as cultivating gratitude and finding meaning in everyday experiences, can help us appreciate the beauty of life and the opportunities we have to make a positive impact. By embracing the idea that what's left when we are gone is the legacy we leave behind, we can strive to create a legacy that reflects our values, passions, and beliefs. In doing so, we can inspire others to live authentically and with purpose, leaving a lasting impact on the world for generations to come.

As we embark on the journey of creating a legacy that transcends death, let us remember that our actions and choices have the power to shape the world around us and leave a lasting impact on future generations. By approaching our legacy-building with intention, reflection, and a commitment to making a difference, we can ensure that our influence lives on long after we are gone. May we find peace in knowing that our legacy is a testament to the love, compassion, and wisdom we have shared with the world, leaving a lasting impact that transcends death.

In the quiet hours of reflection, as we contemplate the finite nature of our lives, the question of what we will leave behind gains profound significance. Creating a legacy that transcends death is not merely about seeking immortality but about committing to a lasting influence that endures beyond our time on earth. This narrative explores how to build a legacy that continues to inspire, uplift, and guide future generations, weaving a thread of enduring impact through the fabric of time.

The journey to crafting a legacy that transcends death begins with a deep understanding of what we wish to impart to the world. This involves a profound self-reflection on our core values, passions, and the unique contributions we are poised to make. It's a path of self-discovery that reveals how we can leave a meaningful imprint on the world that resonates long after we are gone.

Our early experiences and relationships often plant the seeds of our legacy. These formative moments shape our understanding of what is truly important and guide us towards the values and goals we carry forward. Whether it's a mentor whose kindness changed our outlook, a parent who emphasized the importance of integrity, or a pivotal event that altered our perspective, these early influences play a crucial role in defining the essence of our legacy.

For instance, I recall the impact my grandfather had on me. He was a humble man who dedicated his life to helping others in our small town. His quiet acts of service, from fixing a neighbor's fence to volunteering at the local food bank, left a lasting impression on me. Even though he never sought recognition, the ripples of his generosity and kindness influenced many lives, including mine. This early exposure to the power of selfless giving became a cornerstone in my own journey toward creating a legacy.

Defining your unique contribution to the world is central to building a lasting legacy. This contribution is shaped by your passions, the causes you champion, and the distinct ways you make a difference. It's about discovering what sets you apart and how your personal strengths can benefit others.

For me, the realization of my unique contribution came during my years as a teacher. I discovered that my passion lay not just in imparting knowledge but in inspiring curiosity and critical thinking in my students. It wasn't the curriculum itself, but the spark of understanding and the sense of empowerment I could ignite in young minds that mattered. This recognition led me to focus on fostering creativity and confidence in my students, guiding them to explore and develop their own unique potentials.

To create a legacy that transcends death, we must embrace the concept of transcendence—the idea that our actions and influence can extend beyond our physical existence. This involves a conscious effort to invest in endeavors that have a lasting impact and to cultivate relationships and practices that perpetuate our values.

Transcending death through legacy means focusing on actions and initiatives that will continue to benefit others over time. This could be through establishing foundations, supporting causes, or creating works that endure. For example, I decided to start a scholarship fund for underprivileged students who show exceptional promise. This initiative was inspired by my own experience of receiving a scholarship that enabled me to pursue higher education. By providing opportunities to others, I hope to create a ripple effect that extends far into the future, helping students who might otherwise not have had the chance to realize their dreams.

The relationships we build are a vital component of our legacy. They reflect the impact we have on the lives of others and how our values are carried forward. I have found that mentoring young educators and being a supportive friend and colleague have been some of the most rewarding aspects of my life. These relationships are built on trust, mutual respect, and a shared commitment to personal and professional growth. Through these connections, I've been able to pass on the lessons I've learned and the values I hold dear, ensuring that they continue to influence others even after I am gone.

Confronting the reality of our mortality can be a daunting experience, but it also brings a clarity and urgency to our legacy-building efforts. It compels us to focus on what truly matters and to make deliberate choices that align with our vision for the future.

Accepting the inevitability of death allows us to approach our legacy with a sense of peace and purpose. It shifts our focus from fear of the unknown to a commitment to leaving a meaningful mark on the world. For me, this acceptance came through a personal health crisis that forced me to reevaluate my priorities. Facing the fragility of life, I realized that what I wanted most was to be remembered for the love and support I provided to others, for the encouragement I gave my students, and for the positive changes I helped bring about in my community.

Creating a blueprint for a legacy that transcends death involves setting clear intentions and taking actionable steps towards achieving them. It's about making conscious choices that reflect our values and aspirations, ensuring that our influence continues to resonate long after we are gone.

The first step in creating a legacy blueprint is to articulate your intentions. Reflect on what you want your legacy to be and how you can achieve it. For me, it meant clearly defining my goals around education, community service, and personal relationships. I wanted to be remembered as someone who inspired others to learn and grow, who contributed to the well-being of my community, and who lived with kindness and integrity.

With clear intentions in place, the next step is to take action. This involves making daily choices that align with your legacy goals and investing time and resources into initiatives that have lasting impact. In my own journey, this has meant dedicating time to volunteer work, continuing to support my scholarship fund, and actively mentoring others. Each of these actions, no matter how small, contributes to the larger picture of the legacy I wish to leave behind.

Creating a legacy that transcends death is a profound and transformative journey. It's about understanding what matters most to us, defining our unique contributions, and making deliberate choices that reflect our deepest values. By embracing the concept of transcendence, investing in lasting impact, and cultivating meaningful relationships, we can ensure that our influence endures long after we are gone.

As we navigate this journey, let us remember that our actions and choices have the power to shape the world around us and leave a lasting imprint on future generations. May we find peace and purpose in building a legacy that reflects the love, compassion, and wisdom we have shared with the world, creating an enduring impact that transcends death.

Chapter 5: Creating a Legacy that Transcends Death: A Journey of Meaningful Impact

In the ebb and flow of daily life, it's easy to become absorbed in immediate concerns and lose sight of the broader picture. However, at some point, most of us pause to consider what kind of impact we want to leave on the world. This reflection on our legacy can offer a profound sense of purpose and direction, guiding us toward actions and choices that contribute to a lasting positive influence. This chapter explores how we can intentionally shape our legacy to ensure it endures beyond our lifetimes, impacting future generations and reflecting our deepest values and beliefs.

Understanding and setting goals for your legacy is crucial in guiding how you live your life. It involves looking beyond personal achievements and considering the broader impact you want to have. Reflecting on what truly matters to you can help you create a clear roadmap for the legacy you wish to leave.

As you embark on this journey, start by considering the core values that drive your decisions and actions. What principles do you want to be known for? Whether it's kindness, innovation, community service, or something else, aligning your goals with these values ensures that your legacy is authentic and true to who you are. For instance, if compassion is a central value, your legacy might involve initiatives that support vulnerable communities or foster inclusivity.

Setting clear intentions is equally important. Intentions are the compass that directs your actions towards your legacy goals. Whether your aim is to leave a lasting impact on your community, inspire others through your personal story, or be remembered for your integrity, having clear intentions keeps you focused and motivated. For example, I once met a teacher who set an intention to make every student feel valued and capable. Over her career, this intention guided her actions and decisions, leaving a legacy of empowerment and confidence in her students.

To create a legacy that transcends death, it's essential to translate your goals and intentions into tangible actions. Actively engaging with the world around you and striving to make a positive difference is how you bring your legacy to life.

One of the most impactful ways to take action is through volunteering. By dedicating your time and talents to causes that matter to you, you contribute to meaningful change and enrich your own sense of purpose. For instance, I recall a colleague who spent weekends teaching literacy to adults in his community. His commitment not only improved countless lives but also reinforced his legacy as someone who deeply valued education and empowerment.

Advocating for social justice and equality is another powerful avenue for creating lasting impact. Speaking out against injustice and supporting marginalized groups can be challenging, yet it is crucial for fostering a more just and equitable society. I think of an activist friend who tirelessly campaigns for equal rights. Her relentless efforts have not only driven policy changes but also inspired many others to join the cause, amplifying her legacy of advocacy and fairness.

Reflecting on your own life and the legacy you wish to leave is also vital. This introspection can help you understand your motivations and clarify your purpose. By exploring your beliefs and how they shape your actions, you can ensure that your legacy is aligned with your values. A friend once shared how his reflections on mortality prompted him to write letters to his children, expressing his love and sharing life lessons. These letters became a cherished part of his legacy, offering guidance and comfort long after he was gone.

Creating a lasting legacy is not without its challenges. Life's obstacles can test your resilience and determination, but they also provide opportunities for growth and self-discovery. How you navigate these challenges will play a significant role in defining your legacy.

Cultivating a mindset of resilience and perseverance is essential. Instead of viewing challenges as insurmountable barriers, see them as opportunities to learn and grow. For instance, during a particularly difficult period, I learned the importance of adaptability and maintaining a positive outlook. These lessons not only helped me overcome the immediate obstacles but also strengthened my character and resolve, contributing to a more robust and inspiring legacy.

Seeking support from others is equally important. Surround yourself with a network of loved ones, mentors, and allies who can offer guidance and encouragement. During tough times, their perspectives and support can provide the strength needed to persevere. I remember leaning heavily on friends and family during a career setback. Their support was instrumental in helping me navigate the challenges and emerge stronger, reinforcing the value of community and collaboration in my legacy.

Practicing self-care and focusing on emotional well-being are also critical for overcoming obstacles. Taking time to nurture your mind, body, and spirit helps build a solid foundation for resilience. Whether through meditation, exercise, or creative pursuits, these practices can fortify you against life's trials. I have found solace in journaling and meditation, which have not only helped me manage stress but also deepened my understanding of myself and my goals, enriching my personal legacy.

Celebrating Your Achievements and Contributions

AS YOU JOURNEY THROUGH life, it's important to pause and celebrate your accomplishments and the positive impact you have made. Reflecting on these achievements is not just about recognizing your hard work, but also about inspiring others and solidifying your legacy.

Celebrating your successes affirms your worth and value. In the rush of daily life, it's easy to overlook your achievements. Taking time to acknowledge them allows you to appreciate your contributions and the effort that went into them. I vividly remember the first time I received recognition for a community project I led. Celebrating that success not only boosted my confidence but also reinforced my commitment to making a difference.

Recognizing your achievements also highlights the impact you have had on others and the world around you. Whether through your career, personal relationships, or community involvement, each achievement is a testament to your dedication and influence. Reflecting on these moments, I am reminded of how my efforts in organizing local charity events have brought the community together and provided vital support to those in need. These reflections underscore the tangible ways in which my actions contribute to my legacy.

Moreover, celebrating your contributions fosters a sense of gratitude and meaning. It reminds you of the interconnectedness of your actions and their broader significance. This sense of gratitude can bring peace and fulfillment, knowing that you have made a positive difference. Recently, I attended a reunion of volunteers from a project I was involved in years ago. Hearing how our collective efforts had continued to impact lives long after we had moved on filled me with immense gratitude and pride, affirming the lasting nature of our legacy.

Creating a legacy that transcends death is a profound endeavor that involves intentional reflection, purposeful action, and a commitment to making a positive impact. By setting clear goals and intentions, actively engaging with the world, and navigating challenges with resilience, you can craft a legacy that endures and inspires future generations.

As you embark on this journey, remember that you are the author of your own story. Each choice and action contributes to the narrative of your legacy. By celebrating your achievements and appreciating the impact you have made, you affirm your value and inspire others to follow in your footsteps. Embrace the opportunity to shape your legacy with intention and purpose, knowing that your influence can transcend time and continue to make a difference long after you are gone.

Chapter 6: Reflective Practices for Cultivating Gratitude and Meaning in Life

Practicing Gratitude Daily

Practicing gratitude daily is a powerful tool that can transform your life and leave a lasting impact on the world around you. In the hustle and bustle of our daily lives, it can be easy to overlook the simple blessings that surround us. However, taking the time to pause and reflect on what we are grateful for can shift our perspective and bring about a sense of peace and contentment.

Gratitude is not just a fleeting feeling of thankfulness, but a mindset that can be cultivated through daily practice. By intentionally focusing on the things we are thankful for, we can train our minds to see the abundance in our lives, even in the face of challenges and adversity. This practice can lead to increased emotional well-being, resilience, and a deeper sense of connection to ourselves and others.

When we take the time to express gratitude for the people, experiences, and opportunities that have shaped our lives, we are acknowledging the impact they have had on us. This act of reflection can help us gain a greater understanding of our personal legacy and the values that are important to us. By recognizing the contributions of others, we can also find meaning and purpose in our own journey, leading to a more fulfilling and purposeful life.

In exploring spirituality and existential questions in relation to our personal legacy, we may confront our mortality anxiety and fears of what will be left when we are gone. However, by practicing gratitude daily, we can find peace in the knowledge that our legacy is not just about what we leave behind, but also about the impact we have made in the present moment. By living each day with intention and gratitude, we can create a legacy that reflects our values and beliefs, and inspires others to do the same.

In the midst of our fast-paced lives, we often overlook the profound impact that practicing gratitude daily can have on our well-being and the world around us. Gratitude is more than a fleeting feeling of thankfulness; it is a powerful, transformative mindset that can be nurtured through deliberate practice. By cultivating gratitude, we can enhance our emotional health, foster deeper connections with others, and create a legacy that reflects our values and enriches the lives of those around us.

Practicing gratitude daily allows us to shift our focus from what we lack to what we have, fostering a sense of abundance and contentment. This shift in perspective can have far-reaching effects on our mental and emotional well-being, helping us navigate life's challenges with greater resilience and optimism.

Gratitude encourages us to find joy in the simple, everyday moments that we often take for granted. By consciously acknowledging the small blessings in our lives, we can experience a deeper sense of happiness and fulfillment.

I remember a particularly stressful period at work when I began a daily gratitude practice. Each morning, I would take a moment to appreciate the warmth of my morning coffee, the comfort of a good book, or the smile of a colleague. These small acts of appreciation helped me maintain a positive outlook and brought a sense of calm and joy to my day.

Regularly practicing gratitude can also enhance our emotional resilience, enabling us to better cope with adversity. When we focus on what we are grateful for, we build a foundation of positive emotions that support us during tough times.

For example, during a difficult health challenge, I found solace in expressing gratitude for the support of my family and the care of my medical team. This focus on gratitude provided me with the strength to persevere and helped me remain hopeful and positive throughout my recovery.

Building Deeper Connections Through Gratitude

GRATITUDE NOT ONLY enriches our personal lives but also strengthens our relationships with others. By expressing appreciation and recognizing the contributions of those around us, we can foster deeper, more meaningful connections.

When we take the time to express gratitude to the people in our lives, we validate their importance and reinforce the bonds that connect us. This practice can transform our relationships, making them more supportive and fulfilling.

I think back to a time when I made it a habit to thank my team members regularly for their hard work and dedication. This simple gesture of appreciation not only boosted their morale but also strengthened our collective sense of purpose and camaraderie. Over time, these expressions of gratitude created a more positive and cohesive work environment.

Gratitude also plays a crucial role in building a sense of community and belonging. By recognizing and appreciating the efforts of others, we contribute to a culture of mutual respect and support.

In my neighborhood, we started a tradition of community gratitude gatherings where residents share what they are thankful for and recognize the contributions of their neighbors. This practice has brought our community closer together, fostering a spirit of unity and collective well-being. These gatherings remind us of our interconnectedness and the strength we derive from supporting each other.

Daily gratitude practice can lead to profound self-discovery, helping us clarify our values and understand the legacy we wish to leave behind. By reflecting on what we are grateful for, we gain insights into what truly matters to us and how we want to be remembered.

Gratitude helps us identify and affirm our core values. When we consistently recognize what we appreciate most, we gain clarity about what we value and why it is important to us.

During a period of career uncertainty, I began to focus on what aspects of my work I was most grateful for. This reflection revealed that I valued creativity, collaboration, and making a positive impact on others. These insights guided me to pursue a path that aligned more closely with these values, leading to greater personal and professional fulfillment.

By regularly practicing gratitude, we can also define the legacy we want to create. Reflecting on the people and experiences that have positively influenced us can inspire us to contribute to the world in meaningful ways.

As I reflect on the mentors and loved ones who have shaped my life, I am inspired to pay their kindness forward by mentoring others and supporting causes that resonate with my values.

Through these actions, I hope to create a legacy that reflects the gratitude I feel and the positive impact they have had on me.

Confronting our mortality can be unsettling, but practicing gratitude can bring a sense of peace and acceptance. By focusing on the present and appreciating the life we have, we can find solace in the knowledge that our impact continues through the lives we touch.

Gratitude anchors us in the present, allowing us to fully experience and appreciate each moment. This mindfulness helps us to live more fully and find joy in our daily lives, regardless of the uncertainties we may face.

I recall a time of deep personal loss when practicing gratitude for the love and support of my friends and family helped me stay grounded and find moments of peace amidst my grief.

Embracing the present through gratitude allowed me to navigate my sorrow with grace and find meaning in each day.

Leaving a Living Legacy

GRATITUDE TEACHES US that our legacy is not only about what we leave behind but also about the positive impact we create in the present. By living each day with gratitude, we contribute to a legacy of kindness, compassion, and generosity that can inspire others long after we are gone.

One of my neighbors, an elderly woman named Margaret, is a shining example of this. Despite facing numerous health challenges, she always expresses gratitude for the simple pleasures of life and the people around her. Her daily acts of kindness and appreciation have touched many lives in our community, creating a lasting legacy of love and resilience.

Practicing gratitude daily is a transformative practice that enriches our lives and the lives of those around us. It shifts our focus to the abundance and blessings we often overlook, fostering a mindset of positivity and resilience. Through gratitude, we build stronger relationships, clarify our values, and define the legacy we wish to leave.

As we cultivate gratitude, we embrace each moment with a fuller heart and a clearer sense of purpose. Let us continue to express appreciation for the people, experiences, and opportunities that shape our lives, creating a ripple effect of positivity and inspiration. By living with gratitude, we ensure that our legacy is one of love, connection, and enduring impact, transcending the boundaries of time and leaving a lasting mark on the world.

Engaging in mindfulness and meditation is a powerful practice that can transform our lives and leave a lasting impact on the world. In today's fast-paced and chaotic world, it is more important than ever to take a step back and cultivate a sense of peace and presence within ourselves. By engaging in mindfulness and meditation, we can tap into our inner wisdom and connect with our true purpose and values.

Mindfulness is the practice of paying attention to the present moment without judgment. It involves being fully aware of our thoughts, feelings, and sensations as they arise. Through mindfulness, we can learn to let go of negative thoughts and emotions that no longer serve us, and cultivate a sense of gratitude and appreciation for the present moment.

Meditation, on the other hand, is a practice of quieting the mind and connecting with our deeper selves. By taking the time to sit in stillness and silence, we can tap into our inner resources and gain clarity and insight into our lives. Meditation is a powerful tool for reducing stress and anxiety, improving focus and concentration, and cultivating a sense of inner peace and well- being.

Connecting with Others and Building Relationships

IN THE JOURNEY OF LEAVING a lasting impact on the world, one of the most important aspects is connecting with others and building meaningful relationships. Our relationships not only shape who we are, but they also influence the legacy we leave behind. By fostering authentic connections with those around us, we can create a ripple effect that extends far beyond our own lifetime.

Connecting with others goes beyond just surface-level interactions. It involves truly listening to others, empathizing with their experiences, and showing genuine care and compassion. When we take the time to understand and support those around us, we not only strengthen our relationships but also create a legacy of kindness and empathy that will be remembered long after we are gone.

Building relationships is not always easy, especially in a world filled with distractions and busy schedules. However, by making a conscious effort to prioritize our connections with others, we can cultivate a sense of community and belonging that enriches our lives and the lives of those around us. Whether it's spending quality time with loved ones, volunteering in our communities, or simply reaching out to someone in need, every act of connection contributes to our legacy.

In the realm of psychology, self-help, and personal growth, the importance of building relationships cannot be understated. Our connections with others play a crucial role in our emotional well-being, providing us with a support system that helps us navigate life's challenges and celebrate its joys. By fostering healthy relationships, we can find comfort, strength, and inspiration in the face of adversity.

As we reflect on our personal legacy and consider what we want to leave behind, let us remember the power of connecting with others and building relationships. By investing in our relationships and nurturing our connections, we can create a legacy of love, compassion, and understanding that transcends time and space. Let us strive to leave a lasting impact on the world through the power of authentic, meaningful relationships.

Finding Joy and Fulfillment in Everyday Moments

IN OUR FAST-PACED WORLD, it's easy to get caught up in the hustle and bustle of everyday life, forgetting to appreciate the small moments that bring us joy and fulfillment. But it's in these ordinary moments that we can find true happiness and meaning. By slowing down and being present in each moment, we can cultivate a sense of gratitude and contentment that will enrich our lives and leave a lasting impact on the world.

One way to find joy and fulfillment in everyday moments is to practice mindfulness. By paying attention to our thoughts, feelings, and sensations without judgment, we can fully experience each moment as it unfolds. This can help us appreciate the beauty of simple things, like a warm cup of tea in the morning or a smile from a stranger on the street. Mindfulness can also help us cope with mortality anxiety, as we learn to accept the impermanence of life and find peace in the face of death.

Another way to find joy and fulfillment in everyday moments is to cultivate a sense of gratitude. By acknowledging the blessings in our lives, big and small, we can shift our focus from what we lack to what we have. This can help us feel more connected to others and to the world around us, fostering a sense of purpose and fulfillment. Reflective practices, such as journaling or meditation, can help us cultivate gratitude and meaning in life, allowing us to leave a positive legacy for future generations.

In the end, finding joy and fulfillment in everyday moments is about embracing the present moment and living with intention and gratitude. By slowing down, practicing mindfulness, cultivating gratitude, and exploring spirituality, we can leave a lasting impact on the world and find peace. As we reflect on our personal legacy and life reflections, let us remember that what truly matters is how we live each moment with authenticity, compassion, and love.

Conclusion: What We Leave Behind...

AS WE JOURNEY THROUGH life, the concept of "what we leave behind" becomes increasingly significant. This exploration has delved into various facets of legacy—from understanding interconnectedness and the importance of leaving a lasting impact, to practicing daily gratitude and defining a legacy that transcends death. These themes collectively shape our understanding of how to live meaningfully and the imprint we wish to leave on the world.

Our legacy is not merely a footnote at the end of our lives, but a living, breathing entity that we nurture every day through our actions, decisions, and interactions. It's the culmination of the lives we've touched, the changes we've initiated, and the values we've upheld. Whether through grand gestures or small acts of kindness, each of us has the power to create ripples that extend far beyond our immediate sphere of influence.

Understanding our interconnectedness reminds us that our actions don't occur in isolation. Every choice we make, every word we speak, has the potential to affect others in ways we might never fully comprehend. This realization brings with it a profound responsibility—to act with intention, compassion, and foresight.

Practicing gratitude daily not only enhances our own well-being but also contributes to a legacy of positivity and appreciation. By acknowledging the good in our lives and expressing thankfulness, we cultivate an environment of abundance and inspire others to do the same. This attitude of gratitude becomes a part of our legacy, influencing those around us and potentially shaping future generations.

As we contemplate our mortality, we're challenged to define a legacy that transcends death. This involves identifying our core values, pursuing our passions with purpose, and striving to make a difference in areas that matter to us. It's about creating something—be it tangible or intangible— that will continue to inspire, educate, or improve lives long after we're gone.

Ultimately, "what we leave behind" is not about monuments or accolades, but about the essence of who we were and how we lived. It's about the stories people tell about us, the lessons we've imparted, and the positive changes we've set in motion. Our true legacy lies in the hearts and minds of those whose lives we've touched, in the causes we've championed, and in the world we've helped to shape.

As we move forward, let us be mindful of the legacy we're crafting each day. Let us strive to live in a way that aligns with our values, nurtures our relationships, and contributes positively to our communities and the world at large. For in the end, the most profound legacy we can leave is one of love, growth, and positive impact—a legacy that inspires others to live fully, love deeply, and leave their own indelible mark on the world.

In embracing this perspective, we transform our lives from mere existence to a purposeful journey of impact and meaning. We recognize that our time here is finite, but our potential for positive influence is limitless. So let us live each day with intention, kindness, and a commitment to leaving the world a little better than we found it. For in doing so, we create a legacy that truly matters—one that continues to resonate and inspire long after we're gone.

Don't miss out!

Visit the website below and you can sign up to receive emails whenever Samantha Rhodes publishes a new book. There's no charge and no obligation.

https://books2read.com/r/B-A-ERLWB-XHCVD

BOOKS 2 READ

Connecting independent readers to independent writers.

About the Author

Samantha Rhodes is a highly versatile and skilled writer with a rich background in both creative and technical content creation. Known for her dynamic writing style, Samantha has built a reputation for producing engaging, insightful, and well-researched content across a broad spectrum of topics.**Background and Expertise:** Samantha holds a degree in English Literature from a prestigious university, where she honed her skills in narrative construction and critical analysis. Her academic background provided a strong foundation in understanding diverse literary styles and themes, which she seamlessly integrates into her professional work. With over a decade of experience in the writing industry.**Creative Writing:** Samantha's creative work includes short stories, narrative non-fiction, and script writing. Her storytelling prowess allows her to create rich, immersive experiences for her audience. Writing Philosophy: Samantha believes that the key to great writing lies in authenticity and connection. She strives to produce content that not only informs but also engages and inspires. Her meticulous research and commitment to quality ensure that every piece she writes meets the highest standards of excellence.**Personal Life:** When she's not writing, Samantha enjoys exploring new cities, practicing yoga, and indulging in her love for culinary arts. She is also an avid reader, continually expanding her horizons with literature from around the world.